NOV 1 3 2020

DISCARD

D0466511

St. Helena Library
1492 Library Lane
St. Helena, CA 94574
(707) 963-5244

A Gift From
ST. HELENA PUBLIC LIBRARY
FRIENDS&FOUNDATION

More style and less stuff? YES, PLEASE. Myquillyn had me laughing out loud and nodding along as she shared tons of actionable and specific ways to make a home feel welcoming and effortless throughout the entire year—all without breaking the bank.

—SHERRY PETERSIK, *New York Times* bestselling author,
Lovable Livable Home; blogger, Young House Love

Read this book and be set free to listen to the rhythms of the created world and how they inform our homes, our tables, and our everyday lives. Once you embrace this mindset, you'll never, ever go back. More than any other word of advice or expert tip, this book has changed the life of my home, which, in turn, has changed my actual life. Let the seasons be your teacher and Myquillyn Smith be your guide in the only decorating book you'll ever need.

—EMILY P. FREEMAN, *Wall Street Journal* bestselling author,
The Next Right Thing

I trust Myquillyn to style my home any day, but more important, trust Myquillyn to declutter my expectations and perfectionism with her winsome way of pointing us to what really matters. *Welcome Home* is a celebration of the seasons and the way we can all truly embrace each one, right where we are.

—RUTH CHOU SIMONS, bestselling author, *GraceLaced*
and *Beholding and Becoming*; founder, GraceLaced.com

Welcome Home is thick with permission and inspiration, and I'm ready to invite someone over right now. Such a delightful, actionable collection of seasonal magic.

—KENDRA ADACHI, author, *The Lazy Genius Way*

Myquillyn has been reminding us for years that it doesn't have to be perfect to be beautiful. Now she's freeing us up even more with the notion that it doesn't have to be complicated to be festive. Her simple and practical approach to creating a lovely seasonal home is about more than just how our mantels and tablescapes look; it's truly about the art of hospitality. What a gift our dear Nester is to us as we follow her lead in making our homes welcome spaces for gathering, connecting, celebrating, and memory making.

—EMILY LEX, writer and illustrator

Once again, the Nester graces us with perspective shifts that make us want to have everyone we've ever met over for tea. Myquillyn offers so much in-depth goodness in this new book! You will be referencing this for years to come.

—ALLIE CASAZZA, host, *The Purpose Show*

Myquillyn makes it easy! She sets us free to style our homes for each season without driving ourselves—or our families—crazy. Her ideas are simple and doable and will help you welcome guests—and your own family—into the peaceful and beautiful space you've always dreamed of.

—JENNIFER ALLWOOD, business coach;
author, *Fear Is Not the Boss of You*

Myquillyn Smith is the decorating bestie we all need, and *Welcome Home* is the guide we've been waiting for. With vulnerability, gentleness, and quirky humor, this sister-to-all shows us the ropes and proves that they're sturdy. Be gone, intimidation and style paralysis! Creating beautiful, comfy spaces of welcome is more accessible than we imagined.

—SHANNAN MARTIN, author, *The Ministry
of Ordinary Places* and *Falling Free*

Myquillyn's philosophy of "less is more," combined with her imperfection-embracing personality, makes her the home whisperer in my life I never knew I needed. I can attest that this delightful book reflects who she truly is, inside and out—her home has long been a haven for me as a friend. She's the ideal spokeswoman for welcoming, real-life hospitality, all year long, and I'm so glad she's written this book for us.

—TSH OXENREIDER, author, *Shadow and Light*
and *At Home in the World*

Finally: a natural, no-fuss approach to year-round hosting. With her signature wit and engaging style, Myquillyn reminds us that in every season, we don't need a show home in order to show up.

—ERIN LOECHNER, founder, DesignforMankind.com;
author, *Chasing Slow*

WELCOME
HOME

A Cozy Minimalist Guide to Decorating

and Hosting All Year Round

MYQUILLYN SMITH

ZONDERVAN
BOOKS

ZONDERVAN BOOKS

Welcome Home
Copyright © 2020 by Myquillyn Smith

Requests for information should be addressed to:
Zondervan, *3900 Sparks Dr. SE, Grand Rapids, Michigan 49546*

Zondervan titles may be purchased in bulk for educational, business, fundraising, or sales promotional use. For information, please email SpecialMarkets@Zondervan.com.

ISBN 978-0-310-35882-4 (audio)

Library of Congress Cataloging-in-Publication Data

Names: Smith, Myquillyn, author.
Title: Welcome home : a cozy minimalist guide to decorating and hosting all year round / Myquillyn Smith.
Description: Grand Rapids : Zondervan, 2020. | Summary: "Welcome Home is your guide to embracing the four seasons and celebrations at home, with more fun and less fuss. Myquillyn Smith will help you use your home the way you've always dreamed, as you become a hustle-free hostess and infuse your Cozy Minimalist home with simple yet impactful touches that welcome the seasons"—Provided by publisher.
Identifiers: LCCN 2019050491 (print) | LCCN 2019050492 (ebook) | ISBN 9780310351931 (hardcover) | ISBN 9780310351061 (ebook)
Subjects: LCSH: Hospitality. | Minimal design. | Hospitality—Religious aspects—Christianity.
Classification: LCC BJ2021 .S65 2020 (print) | LCC BJ2021 (ebook) | DDC 395.3—dc23
LC record available at https://lccn.loc.gov/2019050491
LC ebook record available at https://lccn.loc.gov/2019050492

All Scripture quotations, unless otherwise indicated, are taken from The Holy Bible, New International Version®, NIV®. Copyright © 1973, 1978, 1984, 2011 by Biblica, Inc.® Used by permission of Zondervan. All rights reserved worldwide. www.Zondervan.com. The "NIV" and "New International Version" are trademarks registered in the United States Patent and Trademark Office by Biblica, Inc.®

Any internet addresses (websites, blogs, etc.) and telephone numbers in this book are offered as a resource. They are not intended in any way to be or imply an endorsement by Zondervan, nor does Zondervan vouch for the content of these sites and numbers for the life of this book.

No part of this publication may be reproduced, stored in a retrieval system, or transmitted in any form or by any means—electronic, mechanical, photocopy, recording, or any other—except for brief quotations in printed reviews, without the prior permission of the publisher.

Published in association with literary agent Jenni Burke of Illuminate Literary Agency, www.illuminateliterary.com.

Cover design: Curt Diepenhorst
Cover photo: Myquillyn Smith
Interior design: Kait Lamphere

Printed in China

20 21 22 23 24 25 26 27 28 29 30 /RRD/ 15 14 13 12 11 10 9 8 7 6 5 4 3 2 1

FOR EMILY

Here's to letting it be easy.

Summer and winter and
springtime and harvest,
sun, moon, and stars in
their courses above
join with all nature in
manifold witness
to thy great faithfulness,
mercy, and love.

—Thomas O. Chisholm,
"Great Is Thy Faithfulness"

CONTENTS

IMPERFECT, SIMPLE ABUNDANCE

> The trickiest thing about writing about hospitality is that it requires using the word hospitality.
> —Shannan Martin, *The Ministry of Ordinary Places*

Yesterday I ran into a Starbucks and even though it's only August 19, there was a sign out front that said "Eight More Days to PSL." That would be the pumpkin spice latte, for those who just woke up from a decade-long coma. Fall is just around the corner, and we the people are counting down the days. That first glimpse of pumpkins and mums at the farmers market is so exciting.

This isn't just fall behavior. If I'm house shopping with a realtor, I point out the perfect spot for the Christmas tree in every house we tour. Even if it's March. Oh, it's March? You'll find me outside in my coat stalking the daffodil shoots with a pair of scissors, waiting to cut that first bloom to bring inside and brighten up my kitchen. I'm almost always looking forward to the next new season, and I adore being surrounded by seasonal goodness in my home. If you're like me, you enjoy looking forward to the change from season to season, and one of the best perks is that you get to add some different seasonal touches to your home. Cue the bins!

Oh, those bins. We've got bins full of cute decor stored away for fall, Christmas, maybe even spring and summer decorating. The stores are on to us. They know we're invested in making sure each season is represented in our homes, and every year they seem to devote more and more square footage to decor for the coming season. It's so easy to believe the lie that stores, Instagram, and Pinterest sometimes whisper that every inch of our homes must be redecorated from top to bottom every three months in order to honor the season.

As much as I want my home to feel connected to the season that's happening outside our walls, I'm not willing to devote more time, money, and storage space than what's needed to get the look I'm craving. I'm guessing you feel the same way. Welp, you've found the perfect companion.

Recognizing each season and letting our homes reflect the seasons as they come is a way to cultivate life-giving homes that feel connected to the world.

This book will completely transform the way you decorate for the seasons. You'll no longer be a slave to bins, your home will feel congruent with each season, and this change will have a profound effect on the way you use your home. What good is a warm, welcoming, pretty home if it's sitting empty all the time?

I find that people like us, who love all this seasonal decorating, are usually the same people who put a high value on the idea of inviting people into our homes. We long for our homes to be ready to host community groups, baby showers, graduations, and of course holiday gatherings throughout the year. Most of us want to get our homes looking the way we've always hoped, not so that we can show off but so that we can use them the way we've always dreamed. As people who value celebrating the seasons with a natural tendency to notice and appreciate the visual, we sometimes put a higher standard on ourselves when it comes to feeling like our homes are ready to open up to people.

If you've ever felt like your home isn't ready for hosting, you are going to be delighted with the connection between creating a seasonal, perennial home and having a hostable home. Recognizing each season and letting our homes reflect the seasons as they come is a way to cultivate life-giving homes that feel connected to the world. To have a seasonal, perennial home means there are certain rhythms throughout the year that dictate how we use our homes and how our homes serve us. It's taken me twenty years to pay attention to how our family uses our home differently throughout the year, but once I was quiet enough to listen, I realized how simple it could be to have a seasonal home. I've learned that when I had the right focus while getting my home ready for each season, I was actually setting it up to make it ready and easy to host. What?! This was the most wonderful discovery!

• • •

It's the same in every episode of *House Hunters*. First comes the not-at-all funny joke about how the wife gets the big closet and the husband will take the micro linen closet in the hall. Then the couple goes on and on about how important it is for them to "entertain." They entertain a lot, so they need a big dining room; they love to entertain, so they need a fun back yard; they've got to have a finished basement because, entertainers. And the show always ends as the couple is slicing cheese and clinking wine glasses with a bunch of friends who look at them and their newly purchased house with admiration.

That's when I look around at the fixer-upper we've lived in for seven years and realize we've never clinked wine glasses over a dining room table filled with assorted cheeses as we entertained admiring friends. I also wonder how often those house hunters entertained friends after the TV crew left town.

We all move into our homes with great intentions to entertain. But entertaining can also feel daunting and grown up and fancy and reserved for people with accents and ascots and maybe yachts. I show off and you sit back and watch, which means the pressure is on me. To entertain means I need to have it all together. Entertaining is all about what I can present to you, and the tricks I can come up with to keep your attention and your admiration.

But here's the thing. For most of us, it's not really entertaining we care about. What we really crave and hope to provide in our homes is hospitality. Hospitality feels welcoming, warm, simple, and as is. It's about mutual receiving. Hosts receive guests into their homes, guests receive care, and both receive connection. Hospitality is grace with throw pillows.

Hospitality is grace with throw pillows.

Entertaining is about the host, but hospitality is about the guest. This makes all the difference for us regular folk, because if we have to wait around until things are perfect to invite anyone over, we'll never do it. But if we choose to make hospitality a priority, we can start right now with whatever we have.

Come as you are, and I'll meet you as I am.

I one hundred percent believe you can invite people over tonight and not even care about the state of your house. You can serve your guests whatever meat will expire tomorrow and have a meaningful, wonderful, great time. I also believe you can throw an elaborate dinner party in which every detail has been

thoughtfully prepared, and do it all in the name of connecting with your guests so they feel honored and loved.

Most of us are looking for something between the last-minute invitation and the fancy dinner. We want our homes to be in a functioning state so it's hospitality ready. The truth is, we won't invite anyone over if we hate the way our houses look. We might feel guilty about it, but we still won't do it. We also want our guests to feel thought of, cared for, and connected with, and we want to easily fit hospitality into our already full lives. We want to be the one who volunteers her home for gatherings and who has just enough of a plan with just enough freedom that doing so doesn't stress her out.

So how do we do that? We start by shifting our mindset.

TWO MINDSET SHIFTS

Two mindset shifts have made all the difference in how I feel about decorating and opening up my home. First, I decided to become an imperfectionist who

believes that my house doesn't have to be perfect to be beautiful. Second, I decided to approach my house as a Cozy Minimalist who understands how to get the most style with the least amount of stuff. I wrote one book about embracing imperfection and another about cozy minimalism, and if you haven't read them, you will love them. For now, I'll give you a quick summary, because understanding and embracing these two mindsets will help you to become the decorator and host you've always known you can be.

The Imperfectionist Mindset

The first mindset shift is becoming an imperfectionist. I confess I came by this mindset the hard way.

Years ago, I more or less told a dear, sweet friend that I absolutely did not trust her. We had just pulled into my driveway after doing something together, and she asked if she could come in and use my bathroom. I told her no. It wasn't because it was messy—I could have run in and grabbed the underwear off the floor. It was because I carried deep shame over the one-hundred-year-old house we rented and the outdated state of it. She and her husband lived in a new house in a nice neighborhood. My house was in the bad part of town, had been a rental for years, and had bright orange Formica counters and a weird bathroom that looked like a serial killer grew up taking showers in there.

I thought I was protecting myself by not letting her come in, but really, by not allowing her to see my bathroom, I was telling her she couldn't be trusted with the imperfections of my life, which is why I went to great lengths to hide them. I was telling her that I expected she would judge me. To this day, I'm still embarrassed to admit that's what I did. I wish I'd had the courage to invite her in. She would not have cared, I would have seen that, it would have solidified our friendship, and I could have started to deal with my perfectionist ways earlier. Instead, I held her art arm's length and we never really got that close.

The truth is, there actually are some people in the world who can't be trusted with the imperfections of my life, but usually, I'm not friends with them. The untrustworthy ones aren't dropping me off at my house with a hug and asking to use my bathroom. Why be friends with people I can't trust to see my mess? If not them, then who?

Hospitality is a high form of trust. It says, *Here's my mess, here are my unfinished things, and here's the truth about me. Knowing you better is worth risking your knowing me better.* Inviting people in is trusting they can handle that. When we open our doors to our friends, essentially we are saying, *Welcome to my home, where things aren't perfect. I trust you can relate.* We tell them to come as they are, and we choose to let them see us as we are.

The great thing about allowing people to see a little imperfection is that it fosters connection. If everyone pretends to be perfect, it's exhausting and surfacey. Once someone goes first and shares something deeper, then a real connection happens and trust begins. Imperfection plays a huge role in our lives, and it's so vital in helping us form healthy relationships that we'd be crazy to banish it.

Becoming an imperfectionist—being able to see the benefits of not trying to be perfect or pretending things are perfect—is the first step to becoming a gracious, others-focused host. Once we realize that we can partner with our imperfections to help us connect with others, it not only changes how we view hospitality, it also changes how we prep our houses. When we believe things don't have to be perfect to be beautiful, the pressure is off. Embracing imperfections and being content with where we are is a great first step to creating the homes we've always wanted so we can use them the way we've always dreamed. But just because we know perfection isn't the goal doesn't mean we don't also need beauty and function.

The Cozy Minimalist Mindset

The second mindset shift that will change the way you approach decorating your home is becoming a Cozy Minimalist.

When we moved into our fixer-upper seven years ago, I knew I needed a logical approach to decorating that solved all sorts of issues. First, I needed to incorporate stuff I already had. This is real life, and there would be no buying a houseful of new furniture like they do on TV. I needed to decide where to focus a limited budget, which meant I needed to prioritize what to tackle first and where to use temporary fixes. And I desperately needed to free myself of a secret hoard of decorative thrift-store finds I had collected over time.

I needed a plan that would allow my style to come through naturally.

I didn't want my love of pretty things to make my life more complicated. I needed to know where to focus my time and money in our home, what to keep and give rid of, and how to do it all based on how our family lived.

I needed the most amount of style with the least amount of stuff. I didn't have time to dust pretend plants, babysit delicate throw pillows, or stand guard over a pristine sofa. I needed a foolproof method I could trust to help me make decisions. Then I needed to apply it and be done enough to relax and finally use our home the way I'd always hoped.

I wanted all the pretty layers and storied goodness a well-lived-in and well-loved-on home has to offer. Give me all the pillows and cushy throws, please. But at the same time, I craved simplicity. The freedom of keeping only what we truly needed, loved, and used sounded extravagant and risky and glorious. Maybe I was a minimalist?

I was intrigued by the possibilities, but then I'd catch a glimpse of a minimalist home that scared me. As enticing as the minimalist movement was, some of those homes seemed like the opposite of inviting. There were no throw pillows, no rugs, no drapes, and no coziness.

I needed a balance of inviting coziness with graceful minimalism. Without purpose, minimal becomes cold and cozy becomes clutter. I was stuck in some weird design space that valued both abundance and simplicity. Both coziness and minimalism. And that's how I became a Cozy Minimalist.

Cozy Minimalists want to live in a world where there is room for plenty. Where meaningful collections are admired and loved and passed on through generations (if they want them). Where parties have oodles of hors d'oeuvres and piles of fruit and cheese on the platter. Where there is more than enough room for us to find a seat and get comfy, and where we, in turn, can share that abundance with others.

But we also love the invitation offered by a cleared-off surface, the freedom not to have to hang something on every wall just because it's empty, the discipline to know when to stop, and the reality that living with less makes our lives so much easier. We need both the cozy and the minimal in our homes. When we decide to be cozy in a minimal way and minimal in a cozy way, we are able to make informed design decisions that create a balanced home. When we embrace the gift of imperfection, we create a graceful home that allows others to connect.

If the idea of minimalism makes you think you'll have to go without, here's another small mindset shift you can make. Instead of focusing on what's lacking, think about minimalism as simply having enough to meet a goal. You and I get to decide on the goals for our homes. That means we can edit out anything that doesn't move us closer to meeting those goals.

When I edited out some things in our family room, the extra space somehow magically translated into space in my life. I started to appreciate walls with less stuff, rooms without clutter, and cleared-off surfaces. Suddenly, home didn't demand extra energy I didn't have. It took less time to clean and gave our family some breathing room. I was captivated by the combination of inviting coziness and graceful minimalism. I learned how to use just the right amount of decor and how to make smart decorating decisions, all through the lens of cozy minimalism.

If I had understood the power of being an imperfectionist and a Cozy Minimalist all those years ago when my friend asked to use my bathroom, I easily could have said yes to her coming in. I would have trusted my friend, and I would have understood that even though I couldn't renovate our rental-house bathroom, there were a few tiny changes I could have made that would have allowed me not to hate that room. I might have been able to like it just by adding a simple white shower curtain, a pretty plant, and a set of cushy towels. But I assumed it was all or nothing, and since I couldn't have an entirely updated bathroom, I had to hide it.

Embracing imperfections makes you a more gracious host to both yourself and others. Becoming a Cozy Minimalist makes you a more confident, balanced decorator. Together, they allow you to get your house looking the way you've always wanted so you can use it the way you've always dreamed.

Most of us aren't trying to make our homes look pretty so our neighbors will be jealous. We want to love our homes so we can use them. We want our homes to look lovely so we can stop thinking about them already. And one simple way we can have homes that look beautiful, fresh, and inviting year round is by incorporating seasonal touches without going overboard. This is your invitation to create some seasonal rhythms of change in your home so it's always ready to welcome you, your family, and your friends.

HOW TO USE THIS BOOK

I wrote this book so you could pick it up and read it one part at a time as each new season comes around. Although, if you want to read it all now, by all means go ahead. But it might feel something like hearing Christmas carols in July. Unless, of course, you live in the southern hemisphere, in which case Christmas and summer weather go hand in hand. Because I live and write in the northern hemisphere, that means readers who live on the other half the world will have to flip the seasons with the holidays. There's no getting around this. Dumb hemispheres messing with this book. My apologies.

The book includes four parts, one for each of the four seasons. Each part includes two chapters—one that focuses on decorating for the season and another that focuses on hosting the celebrations of that season. My hope is that before you unpack that bin of seasonal decor, you'll take a few minutes to read the two chapters dedicated to the season you're about to enter.

Your house might not be perfect, but your hospitality is exactly what we need.

This is your reminder of what to focus on and what not to worry about when it comes to creating a seasonal home that's ready to welcome people.

Simple abundance and imperfection with purpose will be our guides.

There will be no elaborate DIY projects, no precise measurements, no expensive one-time-use party supplies, no servers in color-coordinated outfits holding plates of thirty different appetizers you slaved over.

We don't have time for that.

This is for those of us who want our homes to feel seasonal without taking over our lives. Who want to throw a party so we can laugh with people we love while eating a good meal that didn't take a team of professional chefs to prepare and plan. Who want inviting people over to be so easy that it doesn't require weeks of planning beforehand and multiple naps afterward.

Here's my promise to you: reading this book will not leave you feeling like you have to wait a few more years before you enjoy and open up your unfinished home. Instead, I want you to close this book feeling energized and full of fresh motivation to invite someone over next week.

When it comes to decorating, hospitality, and being okay with your less than perfect home and life, you are ready for this. You don't have to fall into the trap of overplanning, overthinking, overspending, and overdecorating to the point that even the thought of having people over is overwhelming. No. We're gonna keep it so simple.

When it comes to welcoming people into your home, your house might not be perfect, but your hospitality is exactly what we need.

FALL

CHAPTER 1

FALL SEASON

For the Beauty of the Earth

Environment is the invisible hand
that shapes human behavior.
—James Clear, *Atomic Habits*

The opening of Selfridges department store in 1909 forever changed British society. More specifically, it changed the way people shopped.

Pre-Selfridges, the average shop consisted of a tiny storefront with a focused but limited selection of products. Shoppers told the shopkeeper exactly what they needed, were handed their wares from behind a counter, paid for them, and were promptly ushered out once they were finished. Shops weren't for browsing, they were for transactions, thankyouverymuch.

Until Selfridges. On opening day, people from all walks of life were invited inside for as long as they liked. What they saw was a revelation. Instead of a tiny storefront, Selfridges boasted wide-open vistas that created a sense of space and grandeur. Upon entering, customers were greeted with the scent of fresh flowers mixed with the surprising and somewhat uncouth placement of the women's perfume counter front and center. Musicians were brought in and music filled the room. Merchandise displays were artfully stacked and layered, towering on top of counters, beckoning to be picked up. The wares were there to be considered, touched, admired, and of course, purchased.

There were beautiful window displays, playful vignettes, and even an art installation of a hanging crystal swag that threw beams of light all over the hall. The lighting, the placement of every counter, and the floral arrangements all worked together to create not just a place to purchase things but an experience. Selfridge was a master at creating a mood, an atmosphere, a place where people felt welcomed and invited to stay as long as they liked.

Harry Selfridge understood the power of environment and a welcoming atmosphere. He recognized that an environment is more than what the eye can see and that by placing certain things together with intention, he could make people feel welcome. For Selfridge, people feeling welcome in his store led to sales; for us, people feeling welcome in our homes leads to connection. We can give connection a big head start just by the kind of atmosphere we create.

CONSUMER FALL VERSUS CREATOR FALL

After a long hot summer, we're ready for a little chill in the air and a little cozy in our homes. As the stores, magazines, and Instagram fill with beautiful fall decor, we can't help but want to bring some of that fall beauty into our homes. Before you unpack your orange bins or fill up your shopping cart at the nearest craft store, I want you to consider the difference between a consumer style fall and a creator fall. This isn't about right and wrong; it's about intentionality.

Consumer Fall

Have you noticed that fall decor has been a booming business in recent years? Some of us have lost our sanity, filling up every surface with every fall-decor item we can get our hands on. There have been times I've scrolled past a photo on Instagram and couldn't tell whether the room in the photo was a shop selling fall decor or a home in which a family is supposed to live, eat pizza, and fold the laundry—all while working around the pretty fall decor placed on every square inch of visible surface, wall, and seat. More often than not, the space turns out to be a home, not a shop.

Go ahead and take a look at the fall decor hashtags on Pinterest and Instagram. So much of what's there is needlessly over the top. It's as if there's some unspoken contest happening and the person with the most pumpkins on their mantel, porch, or sideboard wins. Guess what they win? A day of packing up fake pumpkins plus a year of storing them in the garage until next fall.

I get it, it's so tempting to think that if one pumpkin is festive, why not use ten or twenty or, by golly, forty-seven pumpkins? I counted pumpkins on an Instagram photo of porch steps one time and there were forty-seven. Forty-seven pumpkins. In another photo, instead of the dining room hutch holding the family's loved-on heirloom serveware with a few nods to fall, it held piles of mass-produced fall dishes with seasonal images and words printed on them—"Pumpkin Spice," "Give Thanks," and of course, "Fall Blessings."

Every corner was packed with store-bought branches, pretend pumpkins, and layers of stuff that would need to be carefully packed away and stored for ten months out of the year, waiting to be unpacked and put on display only for two months every fall.

I admit, I've been fall's worst offender. And it exhausted me.

For years, I believed the consumer fall lie that more stuff means more style. The only way I knew to create a cozy fall home was to buy more factory-produced seasonal decor. So I'd go to the seasonal section of my favorite store and load up my cart hoping that this year, my house would finally feel extra cozy and inviting. I didn't want to spend much money or take too much risk, so I'd buy a bunch of small things. As much as I hated to admit it, all that extra stuff resulted in less style and impact and only added cute-ish clutter. But I was afraid to change. How would my family recognize that it was fall if I didn't have plastic fall trinkets tucked into every corner of the house?

I'm not saying that forty-seven pumpkins on a porch or words on dishes, signs, and welcome mats are bad or ugly. They are not. There's absolutely nothing wrong with store-bought fall decor or piles of pumpkins. But there is

an easier way, one that doesn't rely on packing up bins full of fall-themed wall art, candlesticks, dishes, and rugs.

I love that my family of grown and teenage men still appreciates little details in our home, and there's no way I'm going to let them down when it comes to creating a cozy fall home. But I had to find a way to welcome the season that didn't give me a part-time job of shopping, accessorizing, filling up every surface, taking it all down, packing it away, and storing it just so I could frantically do it all again to usher in the next season.

After moving to and living in fourteen different homes, after twelve years of encouraging women online about all things home, and after writing home books and teaching decorating classes, I've learned there are two types of people when it comes to seasonal decor. There are those of us who have entirely too much seasonal stuff, and then there are those of us who don't have nearly enough. No matter which type we are, we all need to start in the same place. We can take our cues from the one who created fall in the first place.

> We can take our cues from the one who created fall in the first place.

Creator Fall

On any given day, chances are good that you and I could walk outside and immediately know what season it is. I'm not saying that it snows for everyone in the winter. What I'm saying is, no matter where you live, natural rhythms are showing off outside, and if you pay attention, you'll notice them. I've lived in Michigan and the Florida coast and a bunch of states in between. Now I live in North Carolina, and while the leaves are changing here at my house, the grapefruit are getting ripe in Florida. I could still identify the seasons when I lived in sunny Florida; they just had different identifiers. Without even knowing the date, we can know the season because we experience it with our senses. The natural rhythms of creation have been communicating with us through our five senses our entire lives.

Here in North Carolina, I experience autumn in the faded colors, the fallen leaves crunching underfoot, crisp breezes, the smell of a bonfire, and the vivid blue of an October sky. You might experience autumn differently in your region, but you get to decide what feels like autumn to you. In nature, fall isn't overwhelming, chaotic, or stressful. It's about letting go, allowing things to fade, appreciating change, and slowing down.

We don't have to rely on store-bought seasonal decor to create a home that feels like fall, because the best and easiest way to welcome the seasons in our home is the same way we experience the seasons in our everyday lives—through our five senses. When we allow our homes to reflect the season in the same ways that nature is modeling for us, it doesn't take much to make an impact. The simplest, most natural way for our homes to feel like fall is to pay attention to the beautiful yet subtle changes that occur in the world around us and to bring some of that inside.

When I get the itch to change up my house as the season is changing, I go through the same simple routine to remind myself what I really want from my seasonal home. I consider what it is about each season that I love and look forward to, and I do my best to incorporate those things into our home.

This is the starting point for every season, which means if you read this book in one sitting, you may get tired of my bossing you the same way every season. But this is how it works, and we'll do the same thing every season because it makes sense and will work for you. The good news is, you don't have to learn a whole new process every three months—just apply this method to each incoming season.

Begin by gathering some outdoor photos that represent autumn for you. Gathering photos could mean starting an album on your phone with photos you took while walking around your neighborhood. Or it could mean creating a fall-themed Pinterest board of outdoor images that feel autumnal to you. There's no wrong way to do this. Just find a way to collect some fall photos. They might look different from mine, and that's the whole point. If you live in Michigan, you might have photos of orange and red trees; in Florida you might have photos of grapefruit trees heavy with fruit. But just because you live in a certain region doesn't mean you have to focus only on what's happening outside in your area. Even when I lived in Florida, rusty reds and browns felt like fall to me because I grew up in Indiana. All that matters for this practice is that you note the changes in nature that signal fall to you and your family.

Summer into Fall

Before you add things in, it's smart to edit things out. Moving from season to season always starts with removing things first. Walk around your home and remove any summer decor. It's okay if you have some empty space for a while—it's good to let a room breathe a little. In early fall, I'm usually packing up the pool towels and beach bags and the random shells and sea glass we left lying around on lesser-used surfaces. When my boys were younger, I also made room or the homework table for actual homework by storing some of their puzzles and games. Once you've removed summer items and decor, you'll have a clean slate for adding fall touches.

We start with outdoor images because we need to get back to the heart of the season, and that means paying attention to how God decorates first.

My friend Kristen likes to borrow a phrase from "Joy to the World" to describe this step of seasonalizing her home. She says the goal is to let "heaven and nature sing." I love that! We don't have to go around buying and DIYing all sorts of seasonal beauty to fill every surface when we are surrounded by it. Instead, we can find creative ways to bring some of that beauty into our homes each season. Heaven and nature are singing year round, so let's figure out how to incorporate the real stuff of the seasons into our homes.

Then we get to say "enough" and live our beautiful lives moving simply from season to season. My goal is to avoid buying any fall merchandise I have to store. Fall consumables and supplies? Yes. Candlesticks that have the word *fall* painted on them? No. I want to invest in year-round decor I can use in my house in March and November.

So how do we turn inspirational photos of outdoor autumn into real changes in our home?

We work through each of the senses—sight, touch, hearing, smell, and taste.

THE FIVE SENSES OF FALL

Sight: The Look of Fall

When we think of creating a seasonal home, most of us immediately think of all things visual. I'm guessing that like me, you are looking forward to adding some pretty things to look at in your home, and there is so much to choose from. This is the most difficult season for me to keep myself in check, because even though summer is my favorite season to enjoy, fall is my favorite to decorate for, and the stores have figured that out. They know my weakness. So I have to be extra mindful or I'll fill my house with cute fall decor that only gets in my way. One way I put an instant limit on what I bring into my home is by first focusing on a fall color story.

CHOOSE YOUR FALL COLOR STORY. The best way to approach fall decor using sight is to pick a fall color story. A color story is simply a color palette, a set of three or four colors that feel like fall to you. These are the colors you'll want to focus on in making your decorating choices. A color story also helps remind you of what colors not to use so you can instantly pass up some options. It helps you stay focused and make better decisions.

Pay attention to the colors you are drawn to this fall. Look back through those outdoor inspiration photos you gathered and add some more fall photos if you need to. Search a few fall hashtags, such as #falldecor or #autumndecor, and save images that speak to you. Look for images that make you feel cozy and represent what you want to be surrounded by. Then, look over your photos and notice the fall colors you are most drawn to. I find that there are three main color stories that work in the fall. The first is a warm color story with rusty reds, oranges of all shades, and mustard yellows. The second is a cool color story, which might have muddy greens, deep violets, and jewel tones. The third is all about neutral colors like beige, browns, and taupes. There's no right or wrong. Your objective is simply to decide on one color story to use in your home this fall. This will help set some limits on your decision making, and for me, I find it's really helpful to know what colors I can ignore this fall.

Sometimes, I'm drawn to saturated colors. I need deep pinks and orangey-reds in my life, and I don't know why. When that happens, I'm shocked, because it's not what I'm used to or expected. But guess what, since I don't have three bins full of decor that I invested in last year, I'm free to add any fall colors I want to my home this year. And then next year I can do something different if I want. So can you!

Back in the olden days when my boys were little, anyone who wanted a pumpkin that wasn't plain old orange had to drive to the country and hope to find a farmer selling a few heirloom pumpkins. That meant most of us all had the same fall color story—orange with a side of brown and maybe yellow or red for accent colors. Now, however, it's no problem at all to find every size, shape, and color of pumpkin—the real ones—at Walmart. There are elegant white pumpkins with names such as Flat White Boer, Casperita, Moonshine, and Snowball. There are orange-and-yellow-striped Blaze pumpkins, buff-colored Autumn Crown pumpkins, and even the Jarrahdale pumpkins that come in shades of green, blue, or gray. You are so lucky. The pumpkin possibilities are endless! Which means that orange is not the boss of you—unless you want it to be. You can have a warm-toned fall, a cool-toned fall, or a neutral fall with real pumpkins to back it up. Use what works for your home and what feels like fall for you.

When you incorporate a natural fall in your favorite fall colors, it creates that visual difference you are craving after summer but also gives you some lovely limitations so you know what colors to focus on and what not to worry about. When you choose not to depend on store-bought fall decor, you have the freedom to change up your color story every year.

SHOP YOUR HOUSE. One guideline we follow as Cozy Minimalists is always to start with what we have. Once you choose your colors, before going shopping, first shop your house for items in your color story. Walk around your house and look for books, throws, pillows, candles, artwork, dishes, napkins, vases, and throw rugs in colors from your color story. Gather things that might be hidden away on a shelf, behind a cabinet, or in a closet or drawer and bring those items to the forefront this season. Once you do that, you can fill in the gaps by purchasing a few things if you need them. We'll get to that part later. For now, shop the house like a scavenger, hunting for your fall colors.

Shopping your house first helps you avoid buying stuff you don't really need and it also honors the things you already have in your home. As you work through the five senses in this book, I encourage you to always start with what you have, and you might find that your house becomes one of your favorite places to shop.

SHOP YOUR BACK YARD. Before you step into the fall aisles at Target or the craft store, step outside. Be a beauty hunter and see what decor you can find in your back yard. Don't have a back yard? I've been there. There's always a way to shop the outdoors even if you don't have a yard. I've asked neighbors, family members, and even my church if I could cut some branches from the back of their trees and bushes, and in all my years of doing this, no one has ever said no.

You know those annoying trees that won't drop their dried brown leaves until spring? They are my go-to favorites because I can trim a few branches and bring some natural fall into my home without worrying that the leaves will drop. I'll bring a branch or two inside and place it in a heavy-duty vase for instant visual interest.

When my boys were younger, I'd tell them to collect pretty leaves and then we'd decorate them with metallic pens. I used washi tape to tape them up around the house or string them together and hang them from the mantel. This is the least fancy thing in the world, but it feels authentically fall, is fun for the kids, and costs zero dollars for some natural beauty. Even if you don't have a back yard (or kids!), no one will mind if you pick up a few fallen leaves as you walk through your neighborhood or a nearby park. Arrange them in a tray on the coffee table or pile them in a large glass jar for free fall decor.

If you can't bring dried foliage into your home because of allergies, consider putting them on your porch or front steps in a place where you can see them when you look outside. Even a few empty branches without leaves can help a room feel like autumn and last you through Thanksgiving. When it's time to bring out the Christmas evergreen, just throw the stick back out to nature. No plastic bins needed.

EMBRACE THE STATEMENT PUMPKIN. The alternative to realizing you somehow bought thirty-three tiny plastic pumpkins for your dining room table is to focus on one statement pumpkin per room. If you love pumpkins and you are tempted to set out thousands of little pumpkins everywhere, we should be friends, because I'm tempted to do that too.

This year, instead of starting with fake pumpkins, go to the farmers market and look for two or three eye-catching, one-of-a-kind statement pumpkins in your fall color story colors. Do not buy the smallest pumpkin. You are looking for one statement pumpkin that can sit proudly by himself. He needs to be confident and beautiful and the only thing on your kitchen table. Go big and then take him and a few of his siblings home. These pumpkins will last you from September through Thanksgiving. One large real pumpkin is better than fifteen tiny plastic pumpkins. Promise me you'll try it. You'll never go back.

People sometimes challenge me about my preference for real pumpkins. They think they're saving money if they buy a fake pumpkin because they can keep it forever. First, those fake pumpkins aren't fooling anyone. Forgive me, but we both know it's true. Instead of counting the cost of buying a fresh pumpkin or three every year, you also have to count the cost of storing three (or fifty) plastic pumpkins every year. For the price of one pretend pumpkin, I can buy two or three real pumpkins and I don't have to pack them away—praise hands—in an orange bin that cost me ten dollars. I get to spend that money on something else. It's the lazy way out, the smart way out, the

One statement pumpkin per space. They're real, and they're spectacular.

I-might-want-to-change-my-fall-decor-next-year way out. Also, the support-your-local-farmer way out.

One statement pumpkin per space. They're real, and they're spectacular.

Touch: The Feel of Fall

Let's talk about touch, which is next on our list of decorating with the five senses. Fall is all about coziness, which means you want the things people will be touching in your home to be inviting. You're going to use pillows and throws anyway, so take advantage of texture, especially by adding various degrees of nubbiness to your spaces. If you use the same lightweight throw on your sofa year round, it's time for an upgrade. Give yourself permission to find the coziest throw (in a color from your fall color story) for your sofa. In my family, we use a few throws every night in the fall. Instead of a horde of pumpkins, I have three throws that add color and function and coziness to our lives. Functional decor works double duty for you.

Speaking of functional decor, it's time to change the sheets. If silky sheets are cool and inviting in the summer, then fall begs for the coziness of flannel sheets on the bed. Granted, sheets don't meet the technical definition of decor but can contribute to the cozy feel of fall in your home, and that's our goal. You and your family will enjoy seasonal changes like this every single night.

To me, fall feels like bonfires in the back yard with marshmallows on sticks and twinkle lights strung overhead. There is something magical about gathering around a fire with people I care about. It's another reminder that fall isn't cozy because it's full of stuff—we don't need the word *cozy* printed on our marshmallow sticks, do we? It's cozy because it involves people, together-ness, and a real warmth that draws us in. Stuff doesn't define coziness; atmosphere does.

Even if you can't have a bonfire in your back yard, find a way to be near some fire this fall, if only for an evening. Some communities host harvest bonfires, or a nearby apple orchard may have a bonfire and hayrides in the evening.

If you are blessed with a wood-burning stove or fireplace, prep it for the first fire now. Be sure you have something inside and outside for storing wood. Whatever you use inside your home to hold firewood is going to be sitting in your house for the next six months or so. This means you are decorating your house with both wood and whatever is holding the wood, which makes it a nice opportunity to be intentional. Make sure your Firewood Holder Thing™ is something you love looking at. Inspect the stove screen and grate so they are ready for the first fire. Go searching for each piece of the iron tool set that likely got scattered around the house—you'll probably find that tiny fireplace broom in one of the kid's bedrooms. When your wood-burning stove or fireplace is prepped for fires, it will automatically look cozy.

Hearing: The Sound of Fall

Every Christmas, my dad plays the same holiday music. It's an old record his parents used to play at Christmas. For me and my sister, that music *is* Christmas. It's not that we love the particular songs. They are actually kind of weird and one isn't even Christmasy. It's just that through tradition, they've become part of our family's annual Christmas soundtrack. If I'm at the mall and I hear one of those songs, I'm instantly teary with nostalgia for Christmases past.

A similar principle applies to every season. You can fill your home with fall sounds by creating an autumn playlist. You might play the same songs every year as a tradition, or tweak your playlist from one year to the next with a mix of old tunes and new. Take the money you didn't spend on buying more tiny pumpkins and plastic wreaths and use it to deliver your fall playlist into your family's ears. Do you have a way to play music in your home? If not, your job is to make that happen. Providing a decent way to pump some sound through your home all year round is money well spent, and you can use it every day of the year.

Finally, sometimes we don't realize all the noise happening in the background of our lives just because we've grown used to it. From time to time I like to walk around the house and make sure every single noise is turned off. I usually end up giving the refrigerator a dirty look as I realize how loud it can be when it clicks on. I've found bathroom fans running, televisions left on, and once I even had to get rid of a clock because it was entirely too loud. Besides just adding sound to your home, consider whether there are ways you can edit some out.

Smell: The Scent of Fall

Don't underestimate the power of scent. The other day, I was burning a candle when my son walked in from school. The first thing out of his mouth was, "Why does it smell like a doctor's office in here?" I wasn't sure if that was a good thing or if my candle was stressing him out. Clearly, smells stay with us. And what might smell good to one person could smell bad to someone else. Scent won't take up much space, but it covers everything in your home, so use it wisely. Be intentional with candles, essential oils, and fragrant cleaning supplies. An unlit, dusty candle is the saddest thing ever. You do not get to take your unlit candles with you when you die. Burn your candles now. But do be considerate of guests. I like to use my scented items when it's just me and my family, but when we have guests coming, I try not to add any extra layers of scent. Most likely I have something cooking in the oven anyway and I don't want to detract from whatever delicious smell is wafting from the kitchen. Don't underestimate the cozy factor of the scent of cookies baking in the oven or your favorite soup simmering all day in the slow cooker.

While you are gathering up fall supplies in your home, when you are out shopping and are bombarded with fall decor, consider purchasing something that smells like fall to you, and then use it, one scent at a time.

Taste: The Flavor of Fall

Soup, chili, stew, casseroles, breads, roasted vegetables, caramel corn, hot cider, and donuts are undeniably fall foods that we are all ready for after summer. Serving seasonal foods is a delicious way to experience the season. Instead of spending time tweaking and dusting those wooden fall signs on the mantel, bake some bread, make a pot of chili, warm up some apple cider. I promise that your family will love to experience fall through taste. If my boys could choose only one of the senses to focus on for fall, it would be taste. If they could choose two, it would be taste and touch. If they could choose three, it would be taste, touch, and scent. I know that because these are the things in our home that they repeatedly comment on. Visual isn't even in the top three.

Families often have favorite food traditions that signal it's fall. If yours doesn't yet, start some fall food traditions this year. Your family will probably enjoy a delicious fall meal more than another pumpkin on the porch. By the way, do you have all the tools needed to serve your favorite fall meals? I've been in countless homes with an abundance of fall wreaths but not a bread knife to be found. If you're hoping to serve soups and chilis, allow yourself to have the right pots, ladles, soup spoons, and bowls. Now that's a great investment!

FALL SUPPLIES

Once you shop your house, it's time to fill in the gaps by purchasing a few seasonal supplies. Maybe you need some extra decor, or maybe you need some thicker throws or a rug in front of the fireplace. Maybe instead of filling the hutch with plastic leaves, you can fill the air with music that helps create a fall atmosphere. This is how we do fall intentionally as Cozy Minimalists.

Keeping in mind your fall color story, here are a few items to consider as you shop for supplies and welcome the season by focusing on more than just the visual:

Fall isn't about store-bought and factory-made decor. Fall is about cozy togetherness with the people you love.

- Soft, chunky throws in your fall color story colors
- Textured, cushy rugs
- Extra pillows for the sofa and chairs
- Flannel sheets
- Firewood and that Firewood Holder Thing™
- Candles that smell like fall
- Candlesticks that can be used year around
- Essential oils
- Speakers to play your fall playlist
- Seasonal foods like breads, stews, root vegetables to roast, apple cider
- Kitchen tools to make soup, roast vegetables, serve cider, bake cookies

When you embrace autumn in your home through the five senses, anyone who enters will immediately know what season it is, just like in nature.

You don't have to go overboard to have a home that feels like fall. When you focus on simple fall touches that don't require babysitting and storage the rest of the year, you are giving your home, your family, and yourself the gift of less while still embracing all the beauty fall has to offer. Doing fall as a Cozy Minimalist is not about following a set of rules or not being allowed to have certain things. It's the opposite. A Cozy Minimalist welcomes fall with freedom because she knows she's the boss of the stuff in her home.

You get to decide what feels like fall to you, and you get to—no, you *have to*—decide when you have the right amount of stuff. Fall isn't about store-bought and factory-made decor. Fall is about cozy togetherness with the people you love.

CHAPTER 2

FALL CELEBRATION

Blackbird Has Spoken

Celebrations mark the
pinnacles of joy in our lives.
—Ingrid Fetell Lee, *Joyful*

I have lived my entire adult life dreading taking showers. Hear me out—I do in fact take showers. But until I actually set foot in the shower, I try to put off all that work. Just thinking about having to undress, get in the shower, wash and condition my hair, and shave things makes me tired. And that's all just prelude to the real work. We women don't step out of the shower, towel off, put on a shirt and pants, and go. Never. Product in the hair, blow-dry the hair (but not too much), more product in the hair, all while in a tiny bathroom that is now one thousand degrees. More hair product. Next, face stuff. Sunscreen, makeup I'm never quite sure if I'm getting right, and then the fixing of the hair commences. May the odds be ever in your favor. Once I've committed to the work of taking a shower, I can't negate it by wearing my house clothes. I always feel I need to honor all that trouble by putting on actual people clothes instead of yoga pants. Deciding on the shirt-pants-shoes combination takes me longer than I'd like to admit.

The one thing that gets me through and motivates me to take that shower, besides the knowledge that I'll be a social outcast if I don't, is that I have never, not once in my life, regretted taking a shower.

So why am I sharing my shower issues? I'm so glad you asked. Because I experience the exact same feelings when it comes to inviting people over. As the time gets closer to people showing up at my house, I one hundred percent of the time dread that I have to be On. I temporarily hate myself for opening up my big mouth and inviting people to come. Why do I do this to myself? Why can't I just be home alone and watch *Sherlock* again?

It's because I've experienced the truth of hospitality. I have never, ever regretted inviting anyone over. Once it's done, I have never regretted hosting.

Welcoming people into our home has never been a waste of energy, time, or resources. In the same way that God says his word will not return to him void, I'm convinced, through my own highly scientific research, that hosting will not return void to you and me, no matter how much we might dread it before it happens.

FALL FESTIVITIES

There's a reason the chapter about the fall season comes before this chapter about fall celebrations. And I'm going to be saying this every season because it's true: when your home is ready for the season, it's automatically ready for the celebrations within each season. Yep! I tricked you! You thought you were just getting your home all decorated and ready for fall, but really, I was helping you get it done so you could use it to invite people over.

You're welcome.

For those of us in North America, fall has two major events when we might be hosting people, Halloween and Thanksgiving. I know there are differences of opinion about whether to celebrate Halloween, and I am certainly not going to try to talk you into or out of something Halloweeny. But the truth is, if you have kids, they're going to notice Halloween and they're going to want in on the fun. And I, for one, am all about welcoming our neighbors with a bowlful of candy on October 31. Plus, conversation is so much easier when you're wearing an Elvis wig and your neighbor is wearing a cape. My experience with Halloween is that it has been the single most meaningful night of real connection for our neighborhood. This is why we are Team Porchlights On!

A scant three to four weeks later, it's Thanksgiving already. How can we move from late summer into fall, be ready for Halloween, and then welcome Thanksgiving, only to transition into Christmas the very next day? By approaching celebrations as a Cozy Minimalist.

When your home is ready for the season, it's automatically ready for the celebrations within each season.

THE HOSTING TRINITY FOR FALL GATHERINGS

Fall has a big job taking us from summer to pre-Christmas, so as Cozy Minimalists, we want to keep things extra simple. With every seasonal gathering, we'll focus on what I call the hosting trinity—creating a mood, serving food, and, of course, the entire reason we are doing this, which is welcoming people. The mood, the food, and the people are all we need to focus on no matter what kind of gathering we are hosting. If we narrow our focus by paying special attention to these three things, everything else will take care of itself.

Narrowing our focus is important because it's all too easy to feel overwhelmed when we think about hosting, especially for a high-profile holiday like Thanksgiving. Based on what I saw in all the shelter magazines I loved, I used to think legit adult hosting always had to involve real dishes, ironed cloth napkins, breakable glassware, homemade everything, a perfectly styled house and table, and impressive outfits for the whole family. The idea of connecting with others in my home was something I was drawn to, but I didn't have it in me to put on a great show.

But when I thought about times I felt most at home at other gatherings, I realized they didn't look or feel like my image of legit adult hosting. Instead, they were always casual, simple, and informal. The food was approachable, the setting didn't distract from the conversation, and most important of all, I came away from those gatherings feeling more myself, more known, and more connected to others. And so that became my goal for any kind of gathering we hosted, including the high-profile holidays. That's when hosting shifted from feeling overwhelming to feeling more natural, doable, and enjoyable.

Okay, back to the hosting trinity. To make it easy to remember and implement, we'll focus on three ways to add mood, three foods, and three people to consider for any and every gathering you will ever host for the rest of your life. Yep, I promise this works. I use this method whether I'm hosting a thousand people in our barn, thirty people for a graduation party in our back yard, or a few out-of-town girlfriends for dinner in our home.

In each of the seasons, we'll focus on different parts of the hosting trinity. For fall, we are going to focus primarily on the mood or atmosphere. Transitioning from a simplified autumn to a goreless Halloween and then straight into an inviting Thanksgiving doesn't have to feel disjointed. You can do it without having to give your house a makeover three times. We'll use a few simple strategies to help your home move through the seasons smoothly, just as it happens outside in nature.

Mood, food, and people. That's it! Here's how it works.

The Mood: A Goreless Halloween and an Inviting Thanksgiving

A GORELESS HALLOWEEN. Before we moved out to the country, we lived in a close-knit suburban neighborhood where, in the front yards, at least, people decorated for Halloween way more than for Christmas. My three boys were delighted by the inflatable pumpkins, giant light-up spiders, cobweb-covered shrubs, and general creepiness that filled our neighborhood. They wanted to get in on the Halloween fun, and I understood that, but I wanted to find a way to add some fall spookiness without adding a bunch of gore—headstones, skeletons, and fake blood—and also keep things cozy and

minimal. Of course, if gore is your thing, go for it; you can apply the following principles whatever your gore level may be.

In decorating, there is a thing called the rule of three, which simply means that things typically look better in groupings of three. And also it reminds me that three things can have an impact. So, naturally, when it comes to adding some Halloween decor to help create the mood, my advice is to add three Halloweenish items to your home. After reading the last chapter, you already know how to autumnize your home with seasonal elements that cater to the senses. Your home already feels like fall, so you shouldn't feel the need to go over the top. All you need is a little hat tip to October 31st by adding a few low cost Halloween touches your kids are begging for.

I have a wooden candlestick collection I display year round, but it reads differently depending on what I place near it and the candles I use. Come October, I add some drippy black candles and a few black crows from the dollar store. If I really want to up the creepy factor without adding anything that's actually creepy, while I'm at the dollar store I'll grab a few bags of black gauze and or white gauze fabric (sometimes called creepy cloth).

Adding white gauze on dark things, like a dark piece of furniture or the shrubs by the front door, or dark gauze on light things, like the white fireplace, conveys a spooky feel without resorting to blood and guts. So the three things that I use in and around the house are candles, crows, and gauze. Three purposeful items can take a home with your fall color story and a statement pumpkin from a general autumn mood to a Halloween mood without going overboard.

Adding some black gauze to my mantel makes a big spiderwebby statement with a couple of dollars' worth of fabric. The drippy candles and crows satisfy the need for feeling Halloweeny without having to buy fake coffins, severed hands, or other gory props. Use whatever you want to decorate for Halloween, but trust me and see what happens when you choose to simply focus on three places. Adding in some creepy touches that echo the natural world fits with the season and keeps both me and my boys happy. Although I have to admit that now that my boys are older, they don't really care whether I decorate creepy anymore as long as we can watch *Stranger Things* together.

To move from Halloween into Thanksgiving, start by removing anything that is blatantly Halloween. For me, that means removing the black crows and gauze. Depending on how I feel, the black candles might stay or go. You know what the Cozy Minimalist in me loves about this transition? I love that my black crows and gauze can be packed away in something smaller than a shoebox. Be gone plastic jack-o'-lanterns and orange-and-black storage bins! Packing up my Halloween decor takes just two minutes and a gallon Ziplock bag.

With Halloween packed away, it's time to set the atmosphere and decorate for your Thanksgiving gathering. First, take a moment to appreciate the fact that your house already feels and looks like fall with its textured pillows, foraged finds from nature, and your statement pumpkins. Your fall playlist has been filling the house with music for weeks, and of course, the fall foods you're already serving smell and taste delicious. Your house is already well on its way to being prepped for Thanksgiving. You hardly need anything else!

AN INVITING THANKSGIVING. Since you've already seasonalized your home for fall, it's fitting right in with the season. For some of us, that's all we need for Thanksgiving decor. But maybe you want to make your gathering a

A Word about Your Mantel

Does your mantel make a statement? Years ago, I decided it was worth it to find a statement piece for my mantel that I would love and use year round. Once you have your statement piece on your mantel, you won't feel like you have to redesign your mantel every season. And if you love the foundation pieces of your mantel decor, you won't be tempted to add in twenty-seven tiny fall items.

If your mantel has never seemed right, take the time to find a year-round focal piece that can be displayed on it. Here are a few tips to keep in mind as you're searching.

- Aim for something that will fill about two-thirds of the mantel space.
- Try to avoid a piece of art that is covered in glass or mirrored, both of which can sometimes create unwanted reflections. For example, you might love a beautiful mirror only to discover that all it does on the mantel is reflect your ceiling fan. If you would buy a beautifully framed photo of a ceiling fan for your mantel, then go ahead and use the mirror, but otherwise steer clear.
- An architectural piece such as a pair of vintage shutters, a small chippy garden gate, or a decorative wood pediment from an old piece of furniture is often a great choice for a mantel.
- Once you have your statement piece, add a container to hold seasonal cuttings, flowers, or a plant. Then you can switch out the container or add a few seasonal touches to the vignette without having to reengineer your mantel.
- Last, add one element that nods to the season, like a wood candlestick with a black candle or a gourd from the grocery store.

little more special and decorate your home with some additional Thanksgiving touches. No problem!

Once again, we'll use the rule of three. Begin by choosing three places to focus your decorating magic. It could be your front door, your mantel, and your buffet, or your entryway, a windowsill, and your dining table, or any other combination that works for you. Don't go overboard, just pick three places and that's it. You have other things to do besides decorate.

Once you choose three places to add some festive Thanksgiving decor, focus on something large you can add to each space to pretty it up. It's always better to have one large statement item than lots of tiny things spread around. One mistake I often see on Pinterest is focusing too much attention on too many tiny details that just get lost in the room.

Instead of using twelve tiny vases with single stems of flowers, consider a large statement piece such as a basket of mums, a big fall wreath, or an oversized branch with dried leaves tucked into a corner. Focusing all your creative attention into one big, beautiful item makes a bigger impact than gluing one-inch pumpkins onto napkin rings or putting pilgrim stickers on water bottles. Let's commit together never to apply stickers to water bottles again.

Once you've added your Thanksgiving decor, it's time to take stock of utensils, serving dishes, and tableware. Look at the "Hosting Basics" appendix at the end of the book for a reminder of year-round supplies and pull out what you already have. You don't need Thanksgiving specific plates and glassware and serving pieces. You don't need candles with plastic cornucopias glued on. You don't need to switch out your mantel art for Give Thanks art just so you can take it down again in two weeks. Although, I could see Give Thanks art working year round, if you want to work that in.

The Food: Two Foods from Scratch and One Special Drink

Food is the icebreaker of any get together. It's also one of the things we tend to make into a very big deal to the point that it holds us back from inviting people over. Coming up with a menu and then serving it? Going to the grocery store, cooking stuff, making it presentable, and then saving energy to have actual conversations with actual people? Forget it.

Stacked Cider Bar

Supplies

- Apple cider (heated)
- Skewers (I use wooden kabob skewers.)
- Mini pecan pies, mini donuts, or mini cupcakes (Our Walmart carries little 1.5 inch pecan pies which are delightful on a skewer.)
- Apple slices
- Orange slices
- Caramels (Put them at the bottom of the skewer so they melt in the cider. You're welcome.)
- Glass mugs or mason jars (something heavy so the filled skewers don't tip the drink)
- Coffee carafe, crock pot, or Dutch oven to heat and serve the cider
- A ladle to serve the cider
- Optional rosemary for garnish if you want to feel extra fancy

Fill each mug with hot cider, thread the treats on a skewer, and serve with the skewer as a garnish.

When it comes to food, limit yourself to two foods maximum to make from scratch, with the rest being store bought or others brought. This applies even if you are a person who loves to cook—you allow yourself to make only two things. Hosting is about more than just cooking. You need to be in a place where you aren't preoccupied with stirring, basting, timing, and simmering. Make two delicious things and allow the rest to be easy so you can be present.

If you hate to cook, then don't make anything. You can have great food from the grocery store or a restaurant. And remember, people ask what they can bring because they are happy to contribute. Let them bring something and make sure they know it doesn't have to be homemade. And yes, this applies just as much to Thanksgiving with the extended family as it does to Pizza Friday with the neighbors. Never commit to making more than two foods from scratch.

In addition to making only two homemade foods, one thing I love to do that makes my guests feel special and makes me feel like I put thought into having people over is to serve one special drink.

Your guests cannot possibly remember every detail of their time with you, but they will remember something. When you spend a little more time on one lovely detail, you can boss their memory into choosing to remember how delightful that wonderful detail was and how it made them feel loved. I focus on creating one memorable drink because it's a visual delight as well as a taste delight, there's zero cooking involved, and—bonus—everyone gets to drink it. Plus, when you make your special drink a simple but beautiful experience for your guests, no one will remember whether your house needed to be dusted or your tub needed to be scrubbed. I rely on this trick for every gathering I host, no matter the season.

In the fall, my go-to special drink is a stacked hot-cider bar. By "stacked" I mean I stack a bunch of tiny, fall edibles on a skewer and use the skewer as a garnish. It's reminiscent of those over-the-top bloody Marys with the big skewers full of shrimp, peppers, and maybe even a mini sandwich. Only this is a hot, family-friendly drink with fall flavor applied.

Pick one special drink and make it your go-to for the fall. Stock up on supplies and serve it every time you have people over. Your guests will feel special because they get a fun and beautiful drink, and you don't have to worry about special details or garnishes for anything else—the drink does all the wow-factor work for you.

The People: Your Guests, Yourself, and Your People

There are three people to consider every time you host—your guests, yourself, and your people (which includes anyone who lives in your house).

First, you are going to think about your guests. This is the no-brainer, right? Of course you are thinking about your guests—that's the whole reason you invited them over. You want your guests to feel welcomed, thought of, cared for.

The Nest Fest

Seven years ago, Chad and I purchased a fixer-upper on twelve acres outside Charlotte, North Carolina. It had a house I felt we could fix up and live in, but the most important part was the old green, metal tractor barn. Our dream was to fix up it up enough that we could use it to host gatherings.

It's still in desperate need of a million things, but that hasn't stopped us from using it for the past six years. With the help of our family and friends, we've hosted more than five thousand people, most of whom we'd never met until they showed up at our house. It's so important to us to invite people over, into the midst of the mess and undone. And since that's what I'm asking you to do, I feel like I need to be the first to practice it. So consider this your official invitation to our home. We'd love to have you stop by The Nest Fest, held in our back yard in Midland, North Carolina, usually the third Saturday in October. (Google "Nest Fest" or check my blog, thenester.com, for details.) You'll have a chance to sample fare from local food trucks, buy something amazing for your home from the curated vendors, listen to some banjos, and take a moment to connect with us and others in our back yard.

Hospitality is a vital part of who we are, and it's a joy to invite you to our home. Things aren't perfect here, but we trust you can relate. See you in October!

The entire point of having people over is to connect. That's why you care about having cozy places to sit, providing yummy food and drink, and being fully present; they are tools in your connection toolbelt. The goal is to have a deeper, more meaningful connection with anyone you invite into your home. And helping your guests to feel this way means you also need to consider a few other people to make that happen.

Next, you need to consider yourself. A welcoming host is prepared to be present to her guests. That means that helping your guests to feel truly welcome starts with you. Are you ready to listen and engage? Have you arranged your day so you can be fully present and undistracted when your guests arrive? Have you given yourself time and space to prepare so you aren't a ragged, stressed-out mess? If you want to create the worst experience ever for your guests, show up as a distracted, worried host and they'll show themselves out as quickly as possible.

A few years ago, Chad and I met a new couple we had talked about inviting over for months. After lots of back and forth and comparing schedules, we finally found a date that worked for all of us. But the day they were supposed to come over for dinner happened to fall at the end of an unexpectedly hectic and crazy-stressful week for me. Physically and emotionally, I was exhausted and done. The southern lady thing to do would be to push through it all and have these new friends over anyway while I pasted on a fake lipstick smile. Thankfully, I was too tired to even try to fake it, especially with new people. We called and apologized and rescheduled. It wasn't selfish; it was simply the right thing to do. The selfish decision would have been to have them over anyway, knowing I was depleted and had nothing to give. I was in no place to ask good questions, to listen, and to connect. Connection is the point of getting together. I might have been able to pull together a decent meal and a welcoming home, but if there's no room, hope, or energy for connection, then having people over is pointless.

> Welcome people into your home with love, in the midst of the mess, and be human together.

The third set of folks you always need to consider when you invite guests to your home is the other people living in your house. I admit, I have been the worst at this. I sometimes got so caught up in prepping for guests that I'd forget to sit down with my boys and let them know who would be coming and why and what our expectations of them were. So we'd have a great night with friends, but once they left, our boys would be in tears because the Lego Millennium Falcon that they worked so hard to put together six months ago was now in a million pieces all over the floor. That could have been avoided if

I had let them know the ages of the kids coming over and reminded them to put away anything they didn't want those kids to play with.

People are the heart and soul of why we open up our homes. I'm glad you won't make the mistakes I've made in the past when I used to focus on myself and what our guests would think of our home, the food I served, and me. Redirecting your focus to caring for and connecting with others will change your hosting life.

BEAUTIFULLY IMPERFECT

If you follow the hosting trinity formula by focusing on the mood, the food, and the people, your gatherings will be simple, memorable experiences of connection for your guests. This is the kind of hosting that even the host can enjoy. There's no need to turn into a crazy person cleaning every real cobweb only to put up fake ones, feeling like you have to buy a new sideboard before you have guests over, or getting a personal makeover. When I find myself focusing on me, my house, my outfit, or my stuff, it's a red flag.

Hosting is never about the host, and hospitality is never about the house.

If we really believe in the power of imperfections, that they put people at ease and allow us truly to connect, then we won't have to erase all signs of imperfection and real life before we invite people over. We'll realize that sharing some of our everyday imperfection is an essential part of connecting with people. We don't have to finish every project, redecorate every room, overthink or overspend. People remember being loved, welcomed, invited, and thought of. They don't remember whether the coat closet was organized. This fall, let go of the crazy. Welcome people into your home with love, in the midst of the mess, and be human together. Your guests will love you for it.

When we approach decorating, hosting, and life in general as a Cozy Minimalist and imperfectionist, we choose what to focus on and what to let go of. We can't do it all, but we can choose what we can do. So let's create beauty, connection, and meaning with more style and less stuff, with more heart and less hustle. From now, on let's do fall as Cozy Minimalists.

WINTER

CHAPTER 3

WINTER SEASON

While Fields and Floods, Rocks,
Hills, and Plains

'Tis the gift to be simple.

—Elder Joseph Brackett,
"Simple Gifts"

Even though Christmas is about "Emmanuel, God with us," by the looks of my house, you would have thought it was about "Crafting, Hobby Lobby with us," go forth and shop.

Twelve years ago, I made a Christmas garland so colossal and heavy it fell off the wall twenty minutes after I'd put the finishing touches on it. When it fell, it also took part of our makeshift mantel with it. It was my first year blogging, and I had shared with my readers how to make the garland. Full disclosure, I also shared that it fell off the wall, and posted photos to show the carnage.

What I didn't share was how annoyed I was with this garland. Once I put it up, I was committed, but since I didn't like the way it looked when it was just plain greenery, the only solution I could come up with was to make multiple trips to Hobby Lobby to buy more and more stuff to fill it in. All in the name of having a Christmasy home, and all while I secretly longed for simplicity. When it was done, I thought the garland was pretty-ish, but it was so complicated that it required a lot of time to make, and the fake greenery, feathers, and pretend berries cost more than I wanted to spend. Even hanging it took a lot of effort, and then I had to pack it all away just so I could do it again next year. I knew there had to be a simpler way to make my home feel Christmasy. But I was afraid that simpler would mean less festive, and that didn't seem fair to any of us.

I didn't understand that if I had first prepped my home for the winter season, I wouldn't have felt the need to overdecorate for Christmas. If the thought of thoroughly decking the halls has ever felt more like a burden than a blessing, you are going to love taking a seasonal approach this year.

Instead of decorating for Christmas, you're going to focus first on preparing your home for winter. But don't panic. We'll talk about Christmas decor in the next chapter, because for our purposes in this book, we're treating Christmas as a celebration instead of a season. When your home is ready for winter, you'll be freed up to prepare for Christmas in a simpler and more meaningful way. You can winterize your home from Thanksgiving through spring, but Christmas decor is limited to a holiday. Focusing on getting your home ready for winter first means you won't have to exhaust yourself pulling a bunch of storage bins out of the closet or garage only to put them all back three weeks later. Can I get an amen?

CONSUMER WINTER VERSUS CREATOR WINTER

Before you start adding some winter elements in your home, I want you to first think about the two approaches to decorating for every season. Your mindset will guide all of your decisions, so it's really important to start with the mindset that honors your values, beliefs, and goals. Most of us haven't experienced anything other than a consumer winter, especially when it comes to decorating, but there is another option. The still, quiet, unobtrusive creator mindset might be just what you need. I'll let you decide.

Consumer Winter

Sometimes I feel sorry for winter. In a world where the stores seem obsessed with providing us with fall, spring, and summer decor, most overlook winter and focus only on Christmas. Don't get me wrong, I adore Christmas, and as a Christian I'm all about celebrating the birth of Christ. But when it comes to decorating our homes with a seasonal mindset, retailers are taking advantage of the importance of Christmas and hoping to convince us that we need to buy a bunch of stuff to make it special.

We've been trained by stores, advertisers, and, well, even our very own selves to believe that borderline overwhelming is the goal when it comes to decorating at this time of year. And of course the way we try to achieve our winter-wonderlandy, deck-every-inch-of-the-halls goals is by adding layer upon layer of pretty winter and Christmas store-bought goodness.

Over the years, I've relied less and less on store-bought decor, but it's still important to me to have a home that feels seasonal and Christmasy. Here's the secret. God's already laid the groundwork for seasonal change, and it starts with creation.

Creator Winter

We've had only one big snow at our house in the past six years, but after growing up in Indiana and Iowa, nothing makes me feel more wintery than a blanket of fresh snow. I currently live in North Carolina, and even though we don't get much snow in my region, it's cold enough for the leaves to fall, and then the only sign of life left on our property are the Leyland cypress and pine trees.

The empty deciduous trees and brown grass are seasonal reminders of the importance of dormancy and rest. They're also a visual reminder that we are in a season of waiting for something more to come—a season of Advent, of preparation. This is a time when the night is longer, and I remind myself to pay attention to that darkness, to sit with it and let it be instead of instantly trying to banish it by turning on every light in my house. Again, this seasonal darkness correlates with the Advent season as we anticipate and prepare for the coming light of Jesus. I'm not an Advent expert and this book is not the place to go into the liturgical calendar, but I encourage you to consider how the season of Advent can influence your home. If you are already familiar with Advent, be mindful of it as you create your winter inspiration photos.

Fall into Winter

In nature, transitioning from one season to the next is never an abrupt change, and it doesn't have to be in our homes either. I'll buy fall pumpkins for our table as soon as I see them in September and keep them out through Thanksgiving. But the closer I get to Thanksgiving, the more I crave some touches of winter in my home. So I begin to transition by gradually adding some winter to my fall. I might swap out a few gourds and pumpkins for some winter citrus fruit, magnolia leaves, or a few evergreen branches.

I walk around looking for any items I pulled forward to work with my fall color story that don't make sense in winter and put them back in their places. Hoping for one winter snow, I'll go ahead and clean out our boot tray, praying I don't jinx our chances by prepping early for winter weather. I also pay attention to my porch and patio. Now is the time when I pull any plants inside and find a spot for them in the house. Although we use our outdoor patio umbrellas into the fall, I now pack them away for the winter.

Because I do this with every season year round, it feels more like a natural rhythm of considering beautiful and functional seasonal items rather than a Saturday I have to reserve to unpack the new holiday decor. Focus first on the seasons and their supplies, not the holidays and their decor.

If you had a peek at my winter inspiration photos, you would see a dusting of snow on evergreen trees, starry night skies, and leafless trees frosted with ice. Maybe you can relate to this description of winter, or maybe winter looks different to you. Whatever winter represents to you is what matters, which is why, once again, I'm going to boss you into pulling together a little collection of photos, all of which should be images of winter in nature. This is the starting point for every season. Your objective is to train your attention on creation so you can pattern the winter decor in your home on God's winter decor in the natural world. Then you'll be able to welcome winter into your home throughout the entire winter season the same way you experience winter in your everyday life, through your five senses.

THE FIVE SENSES OF WINTER

It's time! I hope this becomes your favorite part of prepping your home for each season. Now consider how you experience winter in nature through the five senses so you can bring some of that into your home through seasonal supplies. Let's get started.

Sight: The Look of Winter

There are three main ways I add the look of winter into my home. And they all, of course, stem from what I see in nature.

SPARKLE. When I think about my visual experience of the winter season, the first thing that comes to mind is light and darkness. The daylight is clearer and brighter and crisper in winter, and a pure and intense darkness arrives in the late afternoon and lingers into the next morning. Even though I am all about sunlight—give me all the sun forever, please—winter reminds me that God created night as well as day, darkness as well as light. I trust that there is divine intention behind the early night blanket full of stars that descends on us before I even have dinner on the table.

And so I choose not to fight creation, which means, like I mentioned earlier, allowing our homes to be darker in the winter. I don't insist that all the overhead lights be on all evening, and I allow for some darker evenings. But I make it a huge priority to incorporate candlelight and sparkle to provide the coziness and touch of delight, wonder, and awe that we all long for during the winter season. I make sure I have the kinds of candles I'll actually burn on hand, paired with a candleholder or container that adds to the winter feel I want. I buy a few packs of tea light candles at the beginning of every winter season, and I shop the house and gather up all my mercury glass votive holders and bring them together to make one big sparkly statement.

I make it a huge priority to incorporate candlelight and sparkle to provide the coziness and touch of delight, wonder, and awe that we all long for during the winter season.

GREENS. Where I live, winter also provides an abundance of evergreen branches, magnolia leaves, and wood. That makes it easy to bring some natural winter greenery into my home. Depending on the climate where you live, your winter greenery might be palm fronds, cypress branches, or buds and flowers off a camellia bush.

No matter where you live, I'm guessing your grocery store carries bundles of evergreen in the floral section—a great way to add some unique greens that you might not have access to in your town. There are online shops like Etsy and Terrain that sell live garlands, swags, and wreaths and deliver them fresh to your door. You can also stop by your Christmas tree vendor and ask if you can grab a few of the cuttings off the ground or from the discard bin to take home. Consider what greens are readily available in nature around you that feel like winter and bring them into your home to help welcome the season. One last note about greens: evergreen is one thing I find myself transitioning out midwinter. Come January, my evergreen branches have seen better days and I'm ready for something fresh, so I trade out evergreens for a pot of paperwhite bulbs from the grocery store or a fresh little plant from the home improvement shop. We'll go into depth about plants in the spring chapter.

NEUTRAL TEXTURE. You don't need to change your style for winter or choose a whole new color story for your home. Unlike fall, where there are a plethora of color combinations in fall decor at the ready that all represent real, natural fall colors, if you really pay attention to winter in nature, you'll notice that things are muted and dry and the color has drained away. Winter color (remember, we're not talking about Christmas yet) is most easily communicated through neutrals and textures. Of course, you can welcome winter with any of the colors of the rainbow, but I've found that to keep things simple, neutral, textural winter decor keeps me happy and works in my home from late November through March.

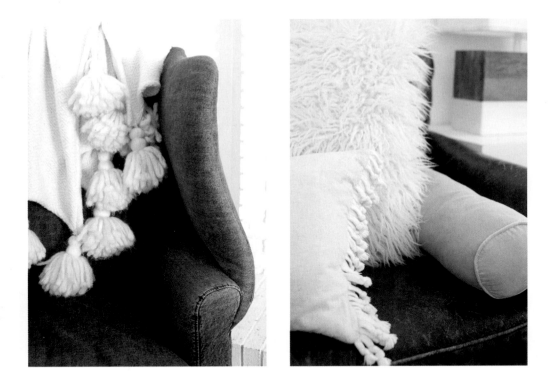

Some examples of textures I like to incorporate in winter are faux furs, blankets, and neutral table runners with decorative tassels or other special details, chunky throws in winter whites, and baskets and wood bowls full of pinecones. Anything neutral, natural, and textural is up for grabs for me to pull out and put on display all winter long. Plus, neutral colors automatically work in any home.

Shop your house and yard looking for sparkle and light, greens and neutral textures. When you shop your own house like a store and pull out winter supplies, you might be surprised at what you already have and how far your everyday items will go to welcome winter.

Touch: The Feel of Winter

In winter, I rely on many of the same elements that create fall coziness, but I try to take them up a notch. I make sure we still have cozy throws on beds and the sofa and switch out fall-colored pillows for textured pillows to snuggle up against. I also love to incorporate a faux fur rug for added texture on a surface or on the back of a chair.

Make sure everyone in your house has warm pj's, house slippers, and a thick soft blanket on their bed. I used to ask my teenage boys if they wanted

Anything neutral, natural, and textural is up for grabs for me to pull out and put on display all winter long.

house slippers and what kind, but I realized that if I asked, they would pass and say they didn't need them and wouldn't wear them. But if a pair of house slippers in their size just showed up in their room every winter, without fail, they all ended up wearing them on cold evenings.

This summer, while sitting in the shallow end of the pool, I read a novel that takes place in the winter in the Pacific Northwest, and every single day, the characters came home from work and built a fire in the fireplace. The nerve! Although we have a working, wood-burning fireplace front and center in our family room where we hang out every night, along with a never-ending abundance of wood from trees that have fallen on our property, for some reason, building a fire feels like the most extravagant, luxurious thing ever. And even though everyone in our family enjoys the heck out of sitting by a real live fire, we don't use our fireplace all that often.

Now that I realize how much I can't wait for winter to enjoy a cozy fire, I'm going to make it as easy as possible for us to store wood, start a fire, and clean up afterward. It is so worth the effort and is part of my annual prepping for winter.

If you don't have a fireplace, you might like this idea: A few years ago we purchased an electric "wood stove," which is simply a space heater placed in a fancier container that looks like a little black stove. It's actually pretty, and when it's really cold and we don't have a fire in the fireplace, we set it right on the hearth in front of the firebox. It creates a ton of heat, but the best part is there's a special lightbulb you put in the back, and when the space heater is on, there's a pretend fire that dances in shades of orange behind the glass window on the front. Even though I know it's a fake fire, the day that lightbulb burned out, I ran out to replace it because that pretend fire added such a cozy ambiance to our home.

More than any other season, winter is the time at our house when we make sure every room is warm and cozy beyond just checking the thermostat. Think about what coziness means to you and your family and make it a priority to sprinkle some cozy into your home this winter.

Hearing: The Sound of Winter

When I think about how I experience winter through what I hear, one thing I think of is a crackling fire. Bonus: if you have a fireplace and use it, you might be hitting more than just the sense of sight but also touch, sound, and smell. Don't have a fireplace? Have you heard of those WoodWick candles? They have a natural wooden wick that sounds just like a crackling fire as it burns. So if a crackling fire is something that sounds wintery to you but you don't have a fireplace, try a WoodWick candle.

You know what else sounds like winter to me? Trains. And not the toy kind that used to encircle the Christmas tree back in the olden days. Remember, bringing the seasons into your home is about what you associate with each season. It so happens that we live around the corner from a railroad line. Although the trains run all year long, I rarely notice the sound of them most of the year. But once it gets cold and the leaves fall, the chugging sounds of trains running the tracks marks time for me all winter.

What sounds like winter to you? Maybe you have a piano. If so, keep it open and inviting and pay the kids five dollars for every Christmas song they learn to play by heart. Author Mary Randolph Carter calls music "the salt and pepper of the home." I love that! Think how bland a meal is without salt and pepper; such is a home without music.

If you started this book with fall or any other season, then you already know that every season requires a playlist. The only difference for winter is that you need to create two playlists: a winter playlist you won't mind listening to in January and February, and a separate playlist for Christmas. You might already have a Christmas playlist, but I want to coach you a little on creating a winter playlist. Consider your winter mood, look again at your inspiration photos, and think about how you feel and what kind of music will enhance your day if you are cooking a pot of soup, watching snow fall, or driving home from work as it's getting dark at 5:00 p.m. I've found I'm partial to slightly melancholy instrumental music during the winter season. So my playlist is full of moody yet ethereal piano and instrumental pieces. You can keep the playlists on your mobile phone or tablet, but play them on speakers for the whole family to hear.

Smell: The Scent of Winter

It's been said that smell can trigger memories. What scents remind you of winters and Christmases past? What scent will your children think of when they think of winter? Essential oils, scented candles, seasonal soaps, fresh pine, cinnamon, hot cocoa, soup, bread, citrus, and the smell of a fireplace or wood-burning stove can transport us to the heart of a wintery experience.

One of the ways we can take advantage of the power of scent is to create a scent rhythm throughout the year. Simply by using a particular scent in your home each season year after year, you can create a signature scent that will remind your family of winter at home. Every winter, I usually burn a vanilla candle on evenings when we are all home. Now that my boys are beginning to move out, I can send a bit of home with them in the form of that same vanilla candle, and they'll think of home every time they light it.

Taste: The Flavor of Winter

Welcome winter though taste. If you've never prepped for a seasonal home through taste, well, start now and your family will thank you.

Every summer, I start to look forward to cooking and eating wintery meals. Comfort food is called that for a reason, and winter is the perfect time to major on providing warm, rustic, comforting foods. If you are cooking for a family, ask what winter foods everyone has been missing. I'm always shocked and surprised by answers like "green enchiladas" and "cheese pie," which is what I called quiche when my boys were little. Even though those foods might not seem wintery to your family, if they are to mine, then that's what I want to make.

Once or twice a winter I decide to go all out and make homemade bread. In my house, a loaf of warm homemade bread is just as rare and valuable as a brick of gold. For years I've followed the simple steps from the cookbook *Artisan Bread in Five Minutes a Day*, and both the process and the result are a winter blessing because the process slows me down and the result tastes delicious. I'm not a baker at heart, but even for this impatient imperfectionist, the bread has always been worth the trouble.

Small things like having individual cocoa packets and a can of whipped cream on hand, or making sure you have a tube of store-bought, "slash and burn" refrigerator cookie dough are simple supplies that delight kids of every age. What foods feel like winter in your home? Do you have what you need to serve wintery meals?

WINTER SUPPLIES

I shy away from holiday-themed items of almost any kind because I'd rather invest in things that can be used all the time. So, no Christmas baskets, vases, or serving pieces for me. Instead of buying Christmas pillows, I look for pillows that feel wintery so I can use them throughout the winter months. Before you pick up any store-bought Christmas decor, first stock up on winter supplies. Here are a few things to look for.

- Candles, sparkly candlesticks, and candleholders
- Music and speakers to play your winter playlist
- Cozy blankets, pj's, and slippers
- Neutral, textured pillows and throws

- Seasonal foods, such as ingredients for cookie dough (or store-bought dough), soup recipes, hot chocolate, citrus
- Evergreen branches mixed in with local greens
- Firewood and anything that makes it easier on you to build a fire

You could shop your house and yard right now and probably come up with most of the items on this list. Once you bring in a few greens, layer out the cozy throws and textured pillows, and toss in a few sparkly, wintery candles, add some music, and bake some cookies in the oven, wouldn't your home feel winter festive? With just a few simple changes, your home will ooze with winter vibes before you even open one red-and-green storage bin.

Before I pull out Christmas stuff, I start to slowly winterize. I don't need to remake the house from top to bottom with all-new, Christmas-approved accessories. I just winterize by catering to the five senses. Plus, once Christmas is over, all of these winter items still make sense in my house. Winterize first, decorate for Christmas second.

Winterize first, decorate for Christmas second.

Starting now, ideally, without cracking open one single Christmas bin, winterize your home. Can you incorporate everyday decor with some natural elements and winter supplies? Buy some things if you need to, but try to purchase items you can use for at least half the year, such as throws and cozy pillows, or all year, such as the ceramic candlesticks you've had your eye on and that wooden serving bowl you'll use at every gathering. Spend your money on candles, good food, hot drinks, and on items you can use in your home for more than the month of December.

Pull out an extra rug to cozy up your wood floors, sprinkle around a dash or two of evergreen and candlelight. Pull out some favorite books and create a warm, inviting atmosphere. Here in the northern hemisphere, winter welcomes Christmas, and winter lasts longer than Christmas, so investing in winter supplies you can use for months is the Cozy Minimalist way.

Once my home is winterized, all I need to do to add a little Christmas is put up a simple tree, hang stockings, and put out the nativity set. We'll talk more about Christmas decor in the next chapter.

CHAPTER 4

WINTER CELEBRATION

Let Us Find Our Rest in Thee

> As we decorate and celebrate, we do so
> to mark the memory of your redemptive
> movement into our broken world, O God.
> —Douglas Kaine McKelvey, *Every Moment Holy*

After more than twenty-two years of momming, I want to tell you a deep, dark holiday secret. More often than not, my boys don't care to help decorate the tree at Christmas. Gasp, I know. Most of the time, I'm alone in the family room untangling lights and picking through broken ornaments by myself while Christmas music plays in the background and my boys play hockey in the street or watch hockey in the basement. And that's okay! I've learned not to force magic moments, not to insist that we all do things together because it's tradition.

When the boys were younger, we did all go together to pick out the tree, and they helped Chad carry it into the house. But once the boys were teenagers, they weren't interested in helping pick out the tree, much less decorate it. Don't tell the Hallmark Channel, but not every family lovingly places treasured ornaments on the tree together while dressed in red-and-green sweaters and sipping homemade hot chocolate.

But let me tell you what we do in fact do together every year. We sit in the glow of the white lights on the tree (Mom decorates, so Mom gets to use the lights she loves) and watch countless Christmas movies together. Everyone enjoys the fact that the tree in the corner is lit and festive and the house finally feels like Christmas. We still have special holiday moments together, but ours just look a little different.

I know your traditions and celebrations look different too. Good for you! Celebrating Christmas doesn't have to look the same as your parents' celebration, a Norman Rockwell painting, or the photos posted by that Instagram influencer you love to hate. The best traditions and celebrations out there are the ones that are meaningful and life-giving and work for your family.

CHRISTMAS FESTIVITIES

If you've winterized your home in a way that welcomes the season with your senses, then your home already feels somewhat Christmasy. Congratulations! Isn't focusing first on seasonal decorating and gathering seasonal supplies the best?!

Now, let's talk Christmas decor and hosting. Since your home is winterized, anyone who enters your home, including you, is already getting cozy winter vibes by what they see, touch, hear, smell, and taste. That means two things: you don't need to pile on loads of additional store-bought decor, and you don't have to deprive yourself of that meaningful beauty you crave that highlights the true meaning of Christmas. The key is to strike the right balance between the two so that decorating for Christmas doesn't become a burden.

If decorating my house for Christmas is a burden, then I stop. I have to. It's the most ridiculous thing in the world to stress out and overdecorate when what I really need is to undo myself and rest in the one whom we are celebrating.

If you are going through the motions this year and decorating the house feels burdensome or unbearable, I beg you, stop. Make a change. Underdecorate, undecorate, settle down. Rest. Isn't that the best atmosphere we can create for our families? We don't need a Christmas that has to be packed away in twenty red-and-green plastic containers and feels like hard work and long to-do lists and hurry. This year, it could be that deemphasizing the holiday decor will help you to reemphasize the true meaning of Christmas. If that's the case, do it. Give yourself the gift of rest by doing less.

Or if this is a year you cannot wait to usher in what "O Holy Night" calls "the thrill of hope," and that means decking the halls, by all means do that! If your decorating and hall-decking energy is high this year, I hope you enjoy every minute of embellishing your home as a visual representation of how you feel about Christmas. There is freedom on both sides of the Christmas

The key is to strike the right balance
so that decorating for Christmas
doesn't become a burden.

decorating spectrum, and both cozy abundance and minimal simplicity can help you celebrate Christmas in your home.

As we talk about readying our homes for Christmas, I'll go ahead and assume you might be hosting something this season. And just as it is with any type of celebration, there are only three things you need to focus on: the mood, the food, and the people. That's the hosting trinity.

THE HOSTING TRINITY FOR WINTER GATHERINGS

The people are always the most important part of the hosting trinity, and the food is often our favorite part, but because Christmas is almost considered its own season, we are going to really focus on setting the mood or atmosphere of our Christmas homes. As a Cozy Minimalist who values both simplicity and abundance with purpose, and as an imperfectionist who is gracious with herself and others, you are already miles ahead of most people who open up their homes at Christmas.

The Mood: Let It Be Simple and Easy

I believe the best gift I can give you is permission and blessing to do less this Christmas. And the weary world rejoiced. Left to my own devices, unchecked and without intention, I usually end up making Christmas more difficult for myself. My default mode is to think I need to do everything the same as I've always done, plus add in fun new ideas I want to try. I assume things need to be complicated and time consuming in order to be special, in order to do Christmas "right." That's the let-it-be-hard mindset, and none of us has time for that kind of crazy at Christmas.

> I believe the best gift I can give you is permission and blessing to do less this Christmas.

Just this year, what if you choose to let Christmas be simple and easy? I know you can't control what your extended family does and the expectations around that. But you can control what happens in your home. What if you demanded less of yourself this year? Start by making some subtractions before you make any holiday additions.

EDIT OUT BEFORE YOU ADD IN. Take a few minutes to walk through each room and remove a few items you don't really need. Extras might include a magazine basket full of last year's reads, the extra clock sitting on your mantel, the stack of decorative books on the coffee table. Whatever it is, aim to make some space by putting a few things away for the holidays. Editing out the extras will give your home some breathing room so it's ready to handle a few choice Christmas decorations.

GIVE YOURSELF BOUNDARIES WITH DECOR. Forget decorating every corner and surface, and choose just three places to focus on. You can make them as overboard or underboard as your energy level and personal style demand. Maybe you need all kid art and color. Maybe you crave all whites and neutrals and hushed tones. Or maybe a nostalgic red-and-green is what your heart desires. Whatever style you want this Christmas, focus your efforts on just three places. Remember, your house is already prepped for the winter season. It's winterized and will carry you until spring. Just add a touch of Christmas in three other places and your home will feel festive.

If one of your three places is the Christmas tree, then you have just two places left to concentrate your efforts. Consider the fireplace, staircase rail, front door,

back door, dining room buffet, an antique mirror, a chandelier, a fun statement piece your home is known for, or a small extra tree filled with Christmas cards from your friends. Once it's winterized, an average-sized home will feel completely festive with Christmas touches at the tree and two other places. Yes, it's true.

Boundaries and priorities are your friends, especially at Christmas. Without them, creating a Christmasy home can easily feel like a burden instead of a gift. And that is the worst.

Here's what boundaries and priorities look like for me. Instead of using eleven strands of tiny twinkle lights for our tree (remember, I'm the one putting the lights on the tree by myself), I can cover the entire tree with just two strands of large, vintage-style C9 Christmas lights. I love the look of the huge white ceramic bulbs! Plus, they give off so much light that the tree is well lit with just two strands. This is fantastic because it makes putting the tree up and taking the tree down so much easier. And if a bulb burns out, no problem! C9 bulbs work like regular lightbulbs and just twist out—no guessing which tiny bulb is on the fritz or replacing fuses. I'm not saying every Cozy Minimalist should use C9 lights, but I am saying every Cozy Minimalist needs to evaluate whether she

is getting the most style with the least amount of stuff, even when it comes to Christmas decor.

Once the lights are up, I finish off the tree with simple ornaments. I add some finger-knit garland my friend Caroline made for me, some pom-pom garland, paper snowflakes the boys and I cut out one year, and some sparkly ornaments for extra glam. We get beauty and meaning without me and my clumsy self carefully unwrapping, wrapping, and storing expensive vintage ornaments every year.

The first year I simplified our Christmas, *Better Homes and Gardens* saw some of the photos I posted and asked to do a Christmas shoot at our house. That convinced me that what I had already experienced was true. I really could have a festive, Christmasy home while using less stuff.

Since I'm not a card-carrying minimalist but a Cozy Minimalist, I get to decide when I've hit my style threshold. At Christmas, I limit myself to three places for decor, but I still like the places I focus on to feel full and abundant. The minimalist part of me keeps the decor simple and doable, and the cozy part keeps things interesting and meaningful.

One last word about boundaries. We probably all have that certain something we want to make sure gets displayed, whether it's a vintage Christmas photo, the nativity set your grandmother gave you, handmade stockings, or a Christmas village collection. Most of us have something that once it's out and displayed, it officially feels like Christmas. Cozy Minimalists are allowed to have collections too, we just understand that the difference between a collection and a hoard is boundaries. So instead of buying every house for the Christmas village forever, we set a boundary. And if we already have too many village houses to fit, we let some go. If you love your Christmas village collection but it's getting out of hand, boss it by setting some limits. Maybe allow only what will fill the top of the piano and nothing more. When you pick the surface first, the boundaries are automatic.

CHOOSE BIGS OVER SMALLS. One of the simplest ways I get more style with less stuff is by using larger items. I talk about bigs over smalls in depth in *Cozy Minimalist Home* and show examples of how I used to decorate my house with one million tiny items only to end up with a home that felt cluttered and disjointed rather than styled.

I've learned the hard way that I can use the same money I would have spent on twelve tiny items to buy one large statement item and get a much bigger return on my investment. Trading out lots of small items for a few big items brings presence and style to my home with less stuff. More style with less stuff is a gift we give to ourselves because it frees us from fussing over our homes so much, especially during the holidays.

Instead of setting out the Christmas salt-and-pepper shakers, the gingerbread-man candy dish, and the Christmas village of twenty-nine tiny houses that now have to be spread around three rooms because they've outgrown their display surface, focus on one large statement piece. Maybe a large wreath of fresh evergreen over your fireplace or on the front door. The added bonus of a fresh wreath is that you get to throw it out at the end of the season. Praises!

If you have a quirky statement piece in your home, it's the perfect place to add a Christmasy touch, since it already demands attention in your home. Add greenery, a buffalo-check bow, or some sparkly ornaments to a place that already draws the eye.

I also love incorporating some large Christmas art in our home. I know it sounds like the opposite of what I say to do for other seasons. Because it is. Doesn't large seasonal art go against everything Cozy Minimalists believe in because it has to be stored away? Yes and no. Here's how I think about it. Christmas is the holiday I decorate the most for anyway. If I have one or two large, lightweight Christmas canvases with words, carols, and verses, packing them up simply means hanging them on a nail where I store my Christmas decor every year. It's an amazing way to get huge style without having to carefully pack away a bunch of small breakables, and it gets much more attention than the twelve five-by-seven prints scattered around the house. If you need big Christmas impact, consider a large canvas from your favorite artist.

The Food: Two Foods from Scratch and One Special Drink

One thing is absolutely for sure. You alone cannot be responsible for every scrap of food this Christmas. You need a plan, and I've got one for you, and you can apply it to every gathering you host.

Pick just two foods to make yourself. The rest needs to be a combination of store bought or others brought. See how it rhymes? That makes it easy to remember. This will save you so much time and energy. You cannot be glazing

a ham, babysitting homemade cinnamon rolls, adding chopped bacon to the green beans, and prepping three appetizers and still hope to have anything left to offer your guests. If you're in robot mode, you'll miss out on the entire gathering. Your guests need you to be present and in an aware state of mind. You can do that only if you give up controlling all the food.

Allow others to help. Allow your favorite restaurant to help. Pick two things you love to make, or two things your guests always rave about, and then buy things that don't matter as much and ask your guests to bring the rest. I don't ask out-of-town guests to bring something unless they are traveling directly from their house to my house and then going home again the same day. But if I have guests staying with me, I'll put them in charge of the appetizers or the drinks or something. Allowing guests to contribute is a way of welcoming them.

People may remember the details from a gathering, but that doesn't mean you have to pay attention to every possible detail in your home. By focusing on a few special details, you get to influence the details that stand out in their memory. No matter what the gathering, the detail I like to focus on is making one special drink.

Christmas Drink Bar

Mocktail Bar for the Whole Family

Supplies

- Clear glasses (mason jars or wine glasses are ideal)
- Ice bucket and ice
- Platter, tray, or wood board to hold fruit
- Clear decanters to hold the juice
- Fun paper straws
- Any type of clear citrus soda
- Two or three types of fruit juice (I try to incorporate different colors.)
- Slices of citrus to squeeze into the drink and use for embellishment
- If you want, set out a chilled crisp or sweet white wine for the adults to mix in.

Usually at Christmas I set up a mocktail bar. We usually have a Christmas Eve brunch with one side of the family and a big dinner with the other. And there are lots of kids around, so I'll grab some Fresca, 7Up, or Sprite and set that out along with two or three different juices poured into glass decanters. I like to use different colored juices like orange, cranberry, and grapefruit because you can mix all sorts of combinations and everyone's drink looks unique. The finishing touch is to pile a bunch of fresh-cut citrus, blood oranges, lemons, limes, grapefruits, and maybe some pomegranates on a pretty plate or wood board so everyone can embellish their drink. Sometimes I'll grab a bottle of moscato or prosecco for the adults to mix in, but for this drink, alcohol is not the focus; enjoying mixing the flavors and choosing your fruit is the fun part.

There might be piles of laundry on the bed and toys on all the stairs, but if you create a delicious coffee bar, a hot chocolate station, or a signature cocktail, your guests will be too busy enjoying their special drink to notice anything else. It's my own hosting secret that I'm hoping you'll try.

When I teach about focusing on a special drink in my classes, I've discovered that there are two types of people: those who love the idea and those who dread it. If you find yourself among the dread-its, you might be thinking you'll just go back to cooking eighty-five foods from scratch instead. Nope! Stop right there. Even if you don't have enthusiasm for a drink station, I promise you someone in your family will. Text your creative sister-in-law or your high-end aunt (come on, we all have both; I'm just calling it what it is), your uncle who loves to entertain, or maybe even your teenage daughter and see if they'd be willing to be in charge of creating a signature drink for your family this year. I'll bet they'll love creating it as much as your guests will love drinking it. Remember, you don't have to do all the things. Ask for help and share the joy of hosting by inviting your guests to contribute.

The People: Your Guests, Yourself, and Your People

I'll remind you of this every season, but the three people you need to be mindful of when you're hosting are your guests, yourself, and the others in your household.

Now it's time to think about how guests are welcomed into your home. You want them to feel at ease and comfortable and loved. A key way to show this is simply by being prepared for them. When you put time and effort into creating a welcoming home where the focus is on connecting with people, it shows. I admit, in the past, my focus on preparing to have people over used to be all about me, my outfit, my house, and getting our family ready so we could be impressive. Or at least not embarrassing. Now, I focus more on what kind of experience our guests will have.

How do you want your guests to feel when they enter your home (no matter the season)? I want our guests to feel relaxed, at ease, and welcomed into a safe and slow place where imperfections are not a surprise, where people are more important than stuff, and where there's room and time for everyone to be heard. I also want to foster connection by providing something we can do together with our guests.

In his book *Get It Together!* interior designer Orlando Soria says to "set the scene, then make a scene." I laughed out loud when I read it. But he's so right. It's one thing to set the scene and get the atmosphere prepped, but it's just as important to create something interesting for your guests to do.

At Christmas, we often have family over who haven't seen each other much during the past year. I try to provide something that acts as an icebreaker to get the conversation going. Depending on the ages of our guests, I'll set out puzzles, coloring books, and markers (for adults too!). I love to plan a simple craft, and so I might set out supplies for making paper snowflakes or materials to make a gingerbread house. I get out old yearbooks, church directories, and photo albums for reminiscing, and set out some musical instruments, board games, and card games for guests to pick up and play. If the weather is decent and there are kids, I like to have some kind of outdoor activity available so they can blow off some steam. Sidewalk chalk, a few balls, or just setting up the fire pit are all great hands-on options. Having options gives guests something

to do and helps create memories. This is especially helpful for little children, because I consider it the worst thing ever if a child is bored at my house, and for teenagers it takes the focus off awkward conversations. No one is forced to join in, but everyone is invited.

One year, we got a new kitten and my nieces were going to be at the house all day. I got each of them a bag of kitten toys so they could play with the new baby cat. In previous years, my nieces and I have made decorative pom-poms and tassels, created essential oil blends, decorated leaves, and learned how to finger knit.

At Christmas, one of my personal rules is that any child coming to my house always gets a gift, even if no one else is exchanging gifts. I try to make sure the gifts are things they can open up and play with right then so it keeps them busy. As much as I like to think my house is a cornucopia of wonderfulness even for kids, I'm sure my younger nieces don't think it's that fun to be in a home that's set up for three teenage boys. No problem, I can solve that with a well-thought-through little gift. My hope is that children always look forward to coming to my house.

> Don't let the day go by in a blurry whirl of activity. Make time to talk and connect.

Last, my sister, Emily, taught me something about gatherings that I always try to incorporate. I call it group time. She says that when a group of people gets together, she always tries to make sure there is at least one group conversation. It doesn't have to be hours long or deep or led by a certified leader. Group time is simply a conversation when everyone is present in the same room, listening to one person talk at a time. This could look like going around and sharing a favorite Christmas memory, sharing something for which each person is thankful, or reading a passage of Scripture or the Christmas story together and talking about it. Ideally, this is a time for everyone to be seen and heard (if they want to be). As the host, it's your job to make sure this little bit of group time happens. It doesn't mean you have to lead it; you can ask the people-person in your family to do that job if you prefer. Just don't let the day go by in a blurry whirl of activity. Make time to talk and connect. I promise it will solidify your time together and make it feel memorable and complete.

Hosting Mindset

How to Know If Your Head Is in the Right Place

- Your pre-celebration thoughts are not focused on what others will think of you
- You've taken a moment (or longer) to relax, breathe, and be still before guests arrive
- You have help; this celebration isn't a one-woman show
- You've considered areas of cozy abundance and allowed for some minimal simplicity in both the decor and food
- You've thought about the people coming and how to best connect with them

To make sure these memorable moments happen, you have to be in a hosting mindset. Years ago, we were invited to dinner at someone's house, and as soon as we got there, it was obvious we had walked into the middle of low-grade chaos. This couple was definitely not in the hosting mindset. The wife had just run out to the store, the husband seemed really flustered, and Chad and I felt like we were in the way. That feeling lasted all evening. It would have been better if they had just canceled at the last minute. In the fall celebration chapter, I mentioned how Chad and I have been on the other side of that dilemma. It's hard to cancel, but better to cancel than to have your guests feel awkward and unwelcome. The entire point of having people over is connection. If you are not in the right frame of mind to do that, then the effort is practically worthless.

But you can't cancel Christmas. So in your preparations, you'll have to prioritize whatever it is you need to do to make sure you can be truly present with your guests. Even if it's running to the bathroom fifteen minutes before

guests arrive, sitting on the bathroom floor by the nightlight, and slowly breathing in and out for a few moments. I have done this myself on many occasions. If you are super prepared, take a few minutes for a slow walk outside and whisper a few prayers before your gathering. It's amazing how slowing down and reminding yourself that the gathering is all about the guests can change your perspective and reduce stress and hurry. You have to have your head in the right place.

Once you've considered your own needs, it's time to consider the others in your household. Over the years, I've learned that it's my job to prepare my family for hosting. Especially my boys. I want them to look forward to having guests and to enjoy their part of hosting. I try to be aware of their personalities and not force them to be someone they're not. For example, one of our boys is like me in his love for people, but also heavy on the introvert side. As an adult, I'm able to balance my week and make sure I have alone time in anticipation of a weekend full of hosting people. But my son doesn't have that option. He's at school all week and looks forward to having alone time on the weekend to play the piano, draw, and read. If I fill up his much-needed alone time with guests, I have to be sensitive to his need to recharge without people around. Instead of insisting that he entertain the other kids nonstop, I make sure he knows he can bow out at some point. I honor his need for alone time before he starts back to school on Monday. Everyone is expected to be kind and interact, but there's room for everyone to do so in a way that honors their personalities.

Remember, even though it's Christmas, perfection is not the goal. By not insisting on perfection for your gathering, you are already lightening your load and being kind to yourself. Instead of perfection, you'll focus on a few important things and let everything else take care of itself. Grace, abundance, presence, and cozy imperfection are your goals.

PACKING AWAY CHRISTMAS DECOR

Once the guests have gone, the used wrapping paper is in the recycle bin, the leftovers are stashed in the fridge, and Christmas is officially over, it's time to take down the Christmas decor. But before you even begin to pack up the

Next year's simple, meaningful Christmas begins now with what you choose to keep in your life for next year. Choose wisely. Your future self will thank you.

lights and the ornaments, you should first set some limits. Decide how much room in your home you are willing to dedicate to storing stuff you can enjoy for just three to six weeks out of the year. Your limit could be a few shelves in the closet, a corner in the attic, or three plastic bins. Decide in advance how much you are willing to store.

Next, open up your storage containers. If you are like me, when you open the storage bins in January to pack away your Christmas decor, there is already stuff in there. What? This is all the decor you didn't use this year because you moved and now your house is smaller and so you don't need it. Or maybe it's the stuff you don't really like but it was a gift, or it's tradition and so you store it forever to avoid the guilt of getting rid of it. Or maybe you just wanted a simpler Christmas and needed to see how it felt not to use every item in your bin. Whatever the reason, if you didn't use that decor this year, that means it's been stored away in your home for twelve months at the minimum. If you avoid getting rid of it now so you can wait until next year to decide whether to keep it, you are storing and lugging out something for years that you don't even know you need. Is it really worth it?

My advice? Keep only the Christmas decor you used this year and give the rest away. When it comes time to pull out those red-and-green bins next year, I don't want you to feel depressed because you have to dig through stuff you don't love. Instead, I hope you open up those bins with joy, enthusiasm, and excitement. Give yourself that gift by deciding now—not next November—what to keep and what to get rid of.

Wouldn't it be nice to look forward to cozying up your home for Christmas without dreading unpacking the decor and then hauling it all back into storage? Wouldn't it be great to open up those bins and love everything you see instead of worrying about how to use what you're tired of? Too often, we get stuck in a forever routine of thinking we have to use everything we have because

that's the way we've always done it. We become rigid taskmasters, all in the name of creating a holiday home. Who wants to hang out with a taskmaster at Christmas? Not me, and not you.

Next year's simple, meaningful Christmas begins now with what you choose to keep in your life for next year. Choose wisely. Your future self will thank you.

BEAUTIFULLY IMPERFECT

When you use the hosting trinity to focus on three places to set the mood, three foods (two from scratch and one special drink), and three people, you can let everything else go and still have a meaningful, memorable gathering that doesn't require a week in hibernation afterward. Over time, as you incorporate this mindset, you'll find yourself thinking less and less about yourself and more about your guests and their experience. You'll become a more confident host because now you know exactly what to focus on and, this is the best part, you also know what not to worry about. When you choose not to force perfection and to allow imperfection to work its magic, people will naturally respond by letting their guard down and connecting on a deeper level. You don't have to have the most festive home on the block in order to host meaningful holiday gatherings. From now on, there will be no more fretting, buying, or DIYing yourself into an exhausted mess before you open your home. People won't remember how impressed they were by your house; they'll remember how impressed they were by your kindness, attention, and openness. This Christmas, welcome people into your home with love and simply celebrate the season together.

SPRING

CHAPTER 5

SPRING SEASON

Morning by Morning,
New Mercies I See

One touch of nature makes
the whole world kin.

—John Muir

I've learned that I start hating our house and property every single March. After a dark season of dormancy and rest during which I am surrounded by acres of leafless trees, grass the color of hay, and lifeless flower beds and borders, I start to feel depressed. This year, I was in such a funk that I put on a dramatic scene in which I broke it to Chad that we simply had to build a garage yesternow to hide our cars because all anyone sees when they pull up to our property is the back of our cars (car butts) under a rickety old carport. And while all of that is true, a scant two weeks later I was so distracted by the peony shoots, blooming daffodils, and fresh layer of mulch tucked in around my flower garden that suddenly—what car butts?

Every single March, spring feels so far away that I don't believe it will ever come again. Maybe this year, there will be no fresh growth. The previous spring happened so long ago that it doesn't seem possible our trees will be green and bushy to the point of intrusiveness again this year. They say it's darkest right before dawn; I say it's most depressing and lifeless right before the buds show themselves. I spend weeks stalking every plant for signs of life, and I start to wonder whether the world was ever as full of green as I remembered it. There's no way the yard in my memory can come from all this brown nothingness. And then, beginning the first week of April, our little corner of the world looks a hundred percent different, with an embarrassment of riches in leafy trees that remain so for the next seven months. Every year, I'm shocked at the abundance of growth, life, and wholeness that seem to happen in a matter of weeks. Half the year we live in Eden, the other half on Mars.

CONSUMER SPRING VERSUS CREATOR SPRING

The onset of spring has me ready to add some much needed life and freshness to my home. But before you and I dive into all things flowers and animal babies, we have to choose our mindset. Are we going to be lured into a consumer spring, or will we focus on a creator spring?

Consumer Spring

In her book *Rhinestone Jesus,* Kristen Welch tells a story of a friend from Kenya visiting their home in Texas. After picking up this friend from the airport, they pull up to Kristen's modest house, the garage door is open, and front and center are the family's five bikes. Of course, everyone in her family has a bike, just as we do. Her friend noticed the bike abundance and was confused. She asked if Kristen and her family owned a bike store—because they had five bikes.

I cannot imagine the confusion this same dear friend might have if she saw some of the spring displays we North Americans have in our homes. Forget about the bike store. Clearly, we must all be running spring decor stores, right?

Because even though one of spring's main selling points is its freshness and natural beauty, leave it to us to ruin that by decorating with plastic everything from the nearest home store.

Too many of us have drunk the proverbial craft store Kool-Aid. We don't even think twice about the ironies of welcoming spring into our homes by adding plastic replicas of nature. We buy plastic birds, branches, bunnies, flowers, chicks, eggs, you name it. Anything we can think of that naturally occurs in spring has been recreated in plastic by a robot and sold to us in a fluorescently lit store aisle. Is this what spring is all about?

Instead of calling plastic decor fake—or it's fancy sister, faux—I refer to it as pretend. It's pretend because using it and believing it's real is a workout for the imagination. We all know there's no way those tulips could survive the night in the wreath on the front door, so we are all silently agreeing to pretend together.

Once again, I admit I have been the number-one target audience for all of it. In the past, the only way I knew to create a pretty spring home was to buy more factory-produced seasonal decor. I'd buy a bunch of small things I could use for only a few months and then store them the rest of the year. I figured I could get lots of figurines and spread them throughout the house, as if I were sprinkling around spring fairy dust. As much as I hated to admit it, all that extra stuff resulted in less style and impact and, once again, succeeded only in adding cute clutter. The spring fairy dust never quite worked its magic.

I'm not saying it's wrong to have a set of three-tiered stands piled high with plastic animals, fabric carrots, wood signs printed with the words *spring* and *bloom*, with pretend flowers and succulents tucked in, all of which needs to be purchased, stylishly displayed for two months, then packed away and stored for ten months to be pulled out again next year. But I did begin to wonder if there might be a better way.

I also secretly wondered whether I needed to be so literal in my love for spring. Was there a way to springify my home without layering groups of pretend plastic everything around my house? Was pretend and plastic really the best way to honor spring?

I longed for a simpler way to have a seasonal home, but I didn't want simpler to mean less springlike. As a Cozy Minimalist, I wanted to welcome spring in a way that didn't require me to live in a pretend plastic world with so much excess stuff, but I still wanted my home to be beautiful.

Creator Spring

In her book *Wild,* Cheryl Strayed quotes her mother as saying, "There's always a sunrise and always a sunset, and it's up to you to choose to be there for it. Put yourself in the way of beauty."

Left to my natural self, I'm more inclined to put myself in the way of Netflix than in the way of beauty. But putting myself in beauty's way is a perspective-shifting practice that grounds me. It needs to be done, and I never regret getting outside, even if that means simply sitting on the porch for fifteen minutes.

> Putting myself in beauty's way is a perspective-shifting practice that grounds me.

I can choose to put myself in the way of beauty. I've decided that it's part of my job as a child of God to do so, to look for beauty in the natural world. It's out there, and sometimes it comes right up and smacks me in the face in the form of a luminous full moon or a sunrise the color of peonies. Sometimes creation is flashy in demanding my attention. Other times, it's quietly there in the background, still putting on a spectacular show, but I see it only when I pay attention. I'm embarrassed to admit that for most of my life, I missed the real show because I was so busy styling my mantel with fabric-and-wire forsythia branches.

When I think about how I truly experience the beauty of spring in nature, it's not really about cute bunnies and nests for me. Instead, I think of new grass that is the most healing color of green, cotton candy clouds, and the awakening of the sky above and the flower buds below.

Spring also represents transition to me. Spring starts out freezing cold and void of life, but it ends up in warmth and a profusion of new life. Spring is like a clean slate, a crisp, fresh start with green shoots. It's hope in bloom. Transitions play out in strong winds, stray snowflakes, vivid blue sky, and sunshine, all of which can happen, where I live, in a twenty-four-hour period.

Spring is all about light. It's getting lighter every day, and many of us get even more of it when we spring forward into daylight saving time. The lightening up of the natural world makes me crave some lightening up of my home.

Welcoming spring into your home begins with considering what spring feels like to you. Once again, your job is to notice what appeals most to you about spring in nature. Even if spring hasn't quite hit your part of the world yet, it's no problem. Simply gather outdoor images of spring on Pinterest or Instagram, or anywhere you can easily access what you've saved. Pay attention to the aspects of creation that trigger thoughts of spring for you. If it's chicks and bunnies, now you know! Noticing what communicates spring to you will help you narrow your focus and decide how to translate those aspects of nature into your home using all five senses.

It's important to do this every season because it helps us practice being intentional. Plus, by thinking about our experience of the season as a whole, we don't limit ourselves to visual decor. Decor can be a great place to start, but when we focus too much on the visual, it's easy to go overboard and cheat the other senses. Ask me how I know.

I was so guilty of going overboard with visual seasonal stuff that I finally decided to get rid of all of my factory-made spring decor and start over. Any decorative thing that felt like it was too literal, too fake, or required too much care went into the giveaway bin. Bye-bye, ceramic bunnies and birds. See ya later, dusty fake nests and bird cages. Farewell, fabric forsythia. The truth is, I never loved those ceramic bunnies, and neither did my boys. I just thought I had to have them because it was spring.

One quick word about all things ceramic bunny. Just because ceramic bunnies don't trigger spring feelings for me doesn't mean you have to feel that way too. If your spring inspiration photos are full of bunnies but you can't have a houseful of real rabbits, then go for it! I think you are the kind of person who deserves a few amazing ceramic bunnies in your house. The point is to welcome spring with intention and purpose, focusing more on supplies you can use no matter the season.

Let your home reflect the fullness of the season in the same ways you experience spring in creation. Pay attention to nature and the beautiful yet subtle changes that occur every year around you. Look at your inspiration images and jot down a few notes about why and how they evoke a feeling of spring in you. Then translate those feelings into your home by considering how you might experience those images not just visually but with all five senses—sight, touch, hearing, smell, and taste.

Winter into Spring

It's time for seasonal editing. Before you and I go adding in a bunch of spring anything, we need to first walk around the house and remove anything that is blatantly winter that we no longer need.

This is usually when I pack away most of my candles and sparkly candleholders.

Scan each room looking for heavy fabric throws, sheets, pillows, rugs, and blankets that can be washed and packed away. If you are still using them because it's cold enough outside to need heavier fabrics, by all means keep them out.

Consider your fireplace. If the weather is already warming up in your region, this might be the time to sweep out the firebox and put the screen, tools, and Firewood Holder Thing™ away until fall.

THE FIVE SENSES OF SPRING

Yay! Here we go, time to work through the five senses and decide what decor and supplies to bring into your home based on how you might experience spring in nature. This practice adds such depth to how everyone will experience your home as it leads you to consider more than just the visual, though the visual is a fun place to start.

Sight: The Look of Spring

Once spring is on the horizon, I begin stalking every blooming tree on our property. As soon as the first flowering tree buds, I'm out there teetering on a ladder, sharp snippers in hand, cutting off a few branches to bring inside. I'm ready for some fresh spring colors. Every shade of pastel catches my eye, whether it be on a pillow, a vase, or a set of dishes. Here's how not to buy a carload of pink everything.

CHOOSE YOUR SPRING COLOR STORY. Vivid colors, pastels, and greens trigger spring thoughts for me. I don't use a rainbow of colors come spring, but I do add in a handful of colors that enhance my current decor.

I also exchange any muted or beigey colors for crisp white. My house is mostly neutral colors with blues, but come spring, I'm craving more color. I love how violet, plum, pink, yellow, or green can enhance my existing color palette in the spring.

> Once spring is on the horizon, I begin stalking every blooming tree on our property.

What colors feel like spring to you? Look back at your spring nature photos to identify the colors that stand out to you. To protect my house from turning into a spring circus, I try to limit myself to adding one main color, like yellow, purple, or pink, along with some greens that are usually represented in plants. Once you decide on the main spring color you want in your home, it's time to shop your house for anything in that color that you can pull to the forefront.

SHOP YOUR HOUSE. Your goal in spring is a fresh start, but that doesn't require redecorating your house from top to bottom. You don't have to switch out everything you have for pastel colors and paintings of flowers. Your objective is simply to enhance your current decor, colors, and style with a few hints that nod to spring. Switching out just a few things you already have for some fresh touches can make a big impact. So skip the spring decor aisle this year and first shop your house for things that feel like spring to you, including items you can enjoy through all five senses.

When you shop your house like a store and pull out spring supplies, you'll probably notice a recurring theme among the things you like. For me, that's plants, white ceramic vases, translucent sparkly glass, watercolor images, and lightweight fabrics. Don't fight your inclinations and style when it comes to seasonal decorating. Take note of them and work with what you already like and have. For example, I've been known to strategically add a stack of colored books to our hutch in April. I tend to change my favorite spring color every year, so sometimes the stack is yellow, sometimes it's pink. The point is,

I already have the books; in spring, I just gather them from wherever they are and group them to add some visual impact. You can do the same by looking for the everyday items in your home that will help you welcome spring, such as candlesticks, throws, pillows, trays, and vases.

LET THE SUNSHINE IN. Come spring, I long for sunlight. I actually sleep more in the winter, maybe you do as well, but by spring, I'm ready to stay up later and get up earlier simply because there's more sunlight every day. I want to soak up every drop of sunshine, and so I make sure nothing is obstructing my windows.

Don't allow dirty windows, drawn shades, or dusty drapes to block your sparkly spring light. I am never more motivated to wash my drapes and dust the blinds than I am in the spring. I've learned that a quick squirt of Windex, even if it's just on the inside of my windows, makes a huge difference in the view. If you have the gumption to wash every window in your house inside and out, by all means, put this book down right now and do it. But if all you can do is set a timer for three minutes and clean the inside of the windows in the main room of your house, I promise you'll see the difference.

Plants and greens are important
to your spring home because
they give it life and freshness.

USE PLANTS—REAL ONES. If you're reading this book at home, look up right now and count how many greens you see. Greens include potted plants, fresh flowers, or something fresh and alive cut from the yard. If all you see is one dusty pretend plant you've had for years, listen up. It's time to buy yourself a real, live plant. This is not an option. I will not have done my job here if you read this book and don't end up with a live plant in your house. Actually, I'd like for you to start with at least one green in every public room. For me, in our public rooms, my goal is to have three greens visible from any vantage point.

We'll talk more about plants and greens in the spring celebration chapter. For now, keep in mind that plants and greens are important to your spring home because they give it life and freshness. Flip through a home magazine and choose a few rooms to focus on. Now, pay attention to the plants, flowers, and cuttings in that room. Count them. Now imagine that room without those greens. Without live greens, those rooms would feel lifeless and unfinished. Without greens, your home might feel the same way.

DO SOME ORGANIZING AND CLEANING. At some point, someone declared spring to be the deep-cleaning season. And if you love to deep clean in spring, can I hire you to come to my house? There are lots of great resources out there for spring cleaning and decluttering, but as a recovering perfectionist, I still tend to avoid starting any project unless I know I can finish it to perfection. Which is great when I'm doing our taxes, but not so great when it comes to deep cleaning the house. So I take my cues from "FlyLady" Marla Cilley, who says, "Housework done imperfectly still blesses your family." As imperfectionists, we don't have to feel bad if we can't clean every square inch of the house from top to bottom; instead, we delight in what we can do, however little.

FOCUS ON TRANSITIONS. In nature, seasons never change abruptly, and so in our homes, we can transition them gradually, just as nature does. Instead of taking an entire Saturday to dewinterize my house just so I can turn around and springify it, I slowly add some spring to my winter by grabbing

Fireplace Filler Ideas

If you have a wood-burning fireplace, it can look like a dump site for ashes by the end of winter. Sweep it out and then add a fern, a stack of painted wood, wood stumps, or large candles—anything to signal that it's no longer the season for fires. Helpful hint: anything white will stand out and become a focal point because it will pop on the black background of the fireplace.

some grocery store tulips when I see them. I also subtract some winter from my spring as the temperature rises by changing out the flannel sheets for regular ones. I do this with every season. Gradually removing a few layers of winter and then adding a few touches of spring is the Cozy Minimalist way. Creation has the right idea with her unhurried pace.

Touch: The Feel of Spring

I know I can't actually reach out and touch spring, but if I could, I think it would feel light and fresh and crisp. Because spring feels crisp to me, I want fewer nubby, fluffy textures. But it's still chilly and we still use throws and blankets in our home, so I'll trade out my faux furs for less textured and lighter throws in colors that feel sharper and more springlike.

Instead of sprinkling around factory-produced decor like fairy dust, consider adding a stack of folded spring throws and lightweight quilts that say spring to you. Switching out wintery pillow covers for spring covers is another simple change that makes an impact, because pillows tend to be things we touch and feel every day.

I once read that the closer an item of clothing is to your body, the more you should be willing to spend on it. (Hello, high-end underwear.) I've decided that the same principle should apply to any decorative items that are closest to our bodies. Even though bed linens and throws might not meet the technical

definition of decor, they are all things our skin touches on the daily, which means we should consider whether they are working with or against the current season. That why I phase out the flannel sheets for crisp percale in the spring. We're all going to use bed linens in our homes anyway, so why not recruit them as spring allies in our seasonal homes?

Speaking of linens, I know people who switch out their drapes in the spring just to change from a heavyweight fabric to a lightweight fabric. Drapes are one way to instantly make a home feel lighter or heavier based on the fabric. You don't have to do this for every window, but it might be something to consider for your main hangout room. Especially if you love change and don't have a bunch of windows.

Hearing: The Sound of Spring

Spring is full of sounds. If it's a warm enough day, open the windows, even if for just an hour, and listen to the birds. After a long winter, birdsong is like therapy.

A few years ago, we got a hammock, and that caused me to spend a lot more time outside—please just ignore everything that that says about me. One thing

I noticed while hammock lounging is how the wind sounds different in spring than it does in winter. In winter, the wind blows through bare tree branches and sounds almost silent; I rarely notice the wind in the winter. But once the leaves on our trees get big enough, the wind rushing through the trees sounds completely different. The first time I hear leafy spring wind, I'm surprised and wonder what in the world that strange, loud sound might be. And then it gives me chills because, oh my gosh, there are leaves on the trees and I can hear them! It's spring! Now the sound of spring wind is part of what signals a new season for me. And just taking a moment to be aware of spring sounds is a relaxing assignment.

We also have a pond on our property that's part of my spring soundtrack. When it gets to be about sixty degrees, the frogs or insects—I truly have no idea what it is making that noise; it could be little fairy people—anyway, whatever lives down there goes crazy, and it's so loud and glorious that we have to turn up the volume on the TV so we can hear it over the pond sounds. The pond in the spring teems with all sorts of life, and when the creatures who live there start their loud chatter, I insist that the porch door stay open. Ten years ago, I never would have left the door open because it somehow feels irresponsible to have my door wide open on a cool spring night. But it's worth it, even if the heat kicks on a little. I figure I can apply all that money I'm not spending on extra seasonal decor to the heating bill.

In addition to making time for nature's soundtrack, I also encourage you to once again create a seasonal playlist. If you're extra ambitious, create one playlist of music with words and another without. I can't think of spring music without thinking of George Winston. His vintage *Winter into Spring* album is full of hopeful melodies that move from melancholy to lighthearted. If you download only one song of his, try "Reflection" or "Blossom/Meadow."

Smell: The Scent of Spring

Just yesterday, I picked up a bottle of spray cleaner I found way in the back of my cabinet. I don't even remember buying it, but when I sprayed it, the floral scent immediately took me back to elementary school and made me nauseated. There was a certain cleaner the school used only when a kid threw up, and this spray smelled exactly like it. So basically, this flowery, clean-smelling spray also smells like barf to me, and I can never use it.

Scent is powerful.

If you walk into a space and there is an obvious smell, whether fantastic or horrible, it's the very first thing you notice. You cannot trick yourself into not noticing a scent. You can get used to it, yes, but you will always notice it at first. You can use this information in your favor as you create a springlike atmosphere in your home.

What smells like spring to you? There's no right or wrong here. Maybe it's flowers, such as jasmine and gardenia and lilac. Or maybe a special dinner of lamb seasoned with mint, rosemary, and garlic is what smells like spring to you. We have lamb once a year at Easter, so the aroma of lamb cooking in the oven is our family's official scent of Easter.

Barf-scented spray cleaner aside, I do try to make cleaning more enjoyable—okay, less of a chore—by treating myself to really-good-smelling supplies and changing the scents often. Thanks to Mrs. Meyer's, I can clean and usher in spring at the same time with lemon-verbena-scented dish soap and radish-scented counter spray. Certain essential oils smell like spring to me, and I save all sorts of oil-blend recipes in a folder on Instagram and refer to them when I want a fresh scent in our home.

And don't you just love the smell of the first freshly cut grass? When an outdoor scent declares it's spring, you could try to replicate it with a candle or room spray, or you could simply open the windows. Or sit out on the porch and take it all in. Let yourself be weird and enjoy a scent you love, even if it makes no sense.

There's a candle company called Homesick that has created a candle scent for every state. Does this mean that every state's scent is heavenly? Nope. It means the manufacturer tried to capture the true scents of each state. Some of their descriptions include words such as "wet road" (Alabama), "a hint of bourbon" (Kentucky), and "grain fields" (Illinois). It was fun doing this high-stakes research and discovering the scents associated with each state. We lived in Iowa for a few years, and my first thought when I went to look at that candle on the website was, "They better try to capture the state fair or else this candle company stinks." (Get it?) Sure enough, the description reads "fragrance that recalls the state fair." Needless to say, I immediately bought that candle and also ordered the Indiana candle ("popped kettle corn"), because that's where

I was born. This company is genius! Not just because all of their candles smell like the best smell ever but because their candles smell like home, which is especially powerful when you no longer live where you grew up.

Don't underestimate the power of smell in creating your spring home. If you get into the rhythm of using certain scents at certain times of the year, including spring, you and everyone in your house will automatically associate those scents with home for the rest of your lives. Use scents to your advantage, and like I suggested before, consider choosing one main scent for spring that you use in your home, whether it's a candle, an essential oil, or a cleaning product, so that every year, when you use it, it will smell like spring no matter what the thermometer says.

Taste: The Flavor of Spring

In our family, the taste of spring is BLTs, salads, asparagus and prosciutto, arugula and goat cheese, lamb, deviled eggs, strawberries, fresh herbs and lemons. Just writing that makes me hungry!

Instead of spending more money on seasonal decor that caters only to the visual and demands to be displayed, consider what tastes like spring to you, and then incorporate that into your menu planning this spring. Food is one of the best ways to invest in a seasonal experience. You have to buy groceries and eat anyway, right? This year, be even more intentional about incorporating seasonal foods into your meals. You get to decide what tastes like spring to you and your people. Over time, you'll create a yearly rhythm that naturally happens just because you cook seasonally.

As a mom to teenage boys, I can testify that if I do nothing but incorporate new scents and tastes of the season into our home, it makes all the difference. If my boys come home from school and I have a fresh candle lit and I'm dipping strawberries in chocolate, you better believe they notice, they comment, they enjoy, and they think the house feels like spring. No decor required.

SPRING SUPPLIES

You could shop your house and yard right now and probably come up with a collection of spring items. I've shifted from stocking my home with store-bought spring decor to stocking it with spring supplies that cater to the five senses. Crisp, fresh colors, lightweight blankets, budding branches, early vegetables, lighthearted music, a bundle of grocery store flowers. Think about it—once you switch out the heavy throws and textured pillows for some spring textures and colors and shop the house to create this atmosphere, would your home feel like spring? Yep, I believe it would.

Before you add in store-bought decor, challenge yourself to celebrate spring with seasonal supplies. Here are a few ideas to get you started.

- Lightweight throws in colors that feel like spring and work with your home
- Potted palm trees, typically available for less than twenty dollars from a big-box or home-supply store
- Multiple house plants with coordinating containers (more about this in the next chapter)
- Tall, narrow vases capable of holding a single budding branch
- White cotton sheets in solids or neutral patterns

This spring, you can create a fresh, life-filled, and life-giving home simply without spending a lot of money. You can incorporate your everyday decor with some natural elements and spring supplies for a fresh look this season. Yes, you are allowed to buy things, but isn't it better to purchase items you can use for longer than a season?

The best part is, once your home is all ready for spring, you've already laid the groundwork for prepping it for others, beyond those who live under your roof, to enjoy. Now that your home is springified, it's practically ready for you to throw open the doors to people for all those wonderful spring gatherings. This is how we welcome the seasons into our homes as Cozy Minimalists.

Crisp, fresh colors, lightweight blankets, budding branches, early vegetables, lighthearted music, a bundle of grocery store flowers.

CHAPTER 6

SPRING CELEBRATION

Then Sings My Soul

> Even a backyard rose
> can be a burning bush.
> —Christie Purifoy, *Roots and Sky*

Every spring for the past five years, my husband, Chad, has hosted an event on our property called Mantime. Forty men from all over the US arrive in Midland, North Carolina, hauling their camping gear. They're willing to use porta-potties and go without showers so they can have a weekend together where the schedule is simple and the conversation is never forced. They eat barbecue, sleep in hammocks tied up all over the place, throw scraps to our rooster, have an evening of "Beer and Hymns," and keep a bonfire going for forty-eight hours straight.

Every single year before it happens, prepping for the event feels impossibly hard. I tell myself it's too much work and the effort isn't worth the results. We are so stupid to host an event like this. This is beyond us. Who do we think we are?

Our property always looks like we must have had a last-minute emergency and didn't get around to getting it ready to host. Chad is usually exhausted from focusing on internet details, answering emails, and doing Costco runs. And it's not a moneymaker for us. We always end up covering extra expenses and footing the bill to make sure the speaker is paid what he deserves. Or at least paid.

Every year, a few guys show up early, and before Mantime even officially begins, they are laughing and connecting. That's when Chad and I forget the impossibly hard stuff leading up to the event and are already convinced of the value of creating a place for people to gather. We should do this more often!

I usually leave and spend the weekend at my parents' house, but a few times I've been around on Friday evening as the banjos and guitars come out and forty men sit in our dimly lit barn singing "I'll Fly Away" at the top of their lungs. It's moments like this when I realize our property was made for this. I would write a check for $10,000 to get the chance to invite these men to our house every year.

Mantime just might be the best thing that happens on this property—not because we do such a great job of managing the details but because we've learned that the most important part of creating a place for connection starts with being willing to open up your mess and invite people into it. We do our part simply by making room and inviting people in.

You might not have forty men camping in your back yard this spring, but I know you value your friendships and you want to be able to have people over without turning into a drill sergeant barking orders to your family and inspecting every inch of your home with a critical eye. As the weather warms up, there are lots of spring holidays and opportunities to open up your home. I want you to be able to volunteer your home with confidence trusting that you won't regret it, knowing that hosting doesn't have to feel like a full-time job.

This spring, you might be hosting an Easter lunch, a baby or bridal shower, a big wedding anniversary, or maybe a book club or Mother's Day brunch. No matter the occasion, there are some proven strategies that will help you host a memorable, beautiful, and practically carefree gathering this spring. It's my job to convince you that hosting guests doesn't have to be stressful or take over your life.

THE HOSTING TRINITY FOR SPRING GATHERINGS

I'm going to remind you of this every season, because with any celebration, no matter what you're celebrating, no matter what the season, there are only three things you really need to focus on: the mood, the food, and of course, the people. That's the hosting trinity. Permission is hereby granted to forget about anything else. Doesn't hosting already feel easier?

The Mood: Simplify and Add Life

The mood or atmosphere is the general feeling you have when you walk into a space. A Cozy Minimalist values both simplicity and abundance with purpose. An imperfectionist is full of grace for herself, for her home, and for others. I don't know about you, but that's the kind of host I hope plans every event, gathering, and dinner I attend for the rest of my life. You are already so far ahead of most people when it comes to creating an inviting mood.

Now let's talk about creating a spring mood for your guests. If you followed through on using the five senses to bring spring into your home, then your home is practically guest-ready as is. Just by walking in, your guests will know it's springtime by what they see, feel, hear, smell, and taste. You don't need to overcompensate with store-bought spring decor, but you also don't need to deprive your home of meaningful beauty that highlights the freshness of the season.

Before inviting people over in the spring, I focus on just two things in my home: simplifying and adding life. If you do nothing else, these will serve you so well.

SIMPLIFY SURFACES WITH A HOME BASE. Every spring, I simplify all of our surfaces. I call it a surface cleanse. Around this time every year, I realize I have stuff buildup. So I usually spend some time simplifying my decor, and then come summer, fall, and winter, my surfaces slowly accumulate more stuff. If I don't destufficate, then I never have a fresh start, and that's one of spring's main taglines.

Focus on the most sought-after surfaces in your home, such as the kitchen island and counters, the breakfast table, maybe the dressers, coffee table, sideboards, anything visible that sits out, especially in the public rooms. Any surface that seems to just beg your family to set their stuff on it every day.

Something magical happened when I prioritized a cleared off surface.

Find a temporary holding place to set all of your surface decor and stuff. You can leave the lamps on your surfaces and anything that a hundred percent gets used daily, such as the coffee maker, but everything else should be removed during this quick process. Next, get your steamy-hot rag and some cleaner that smells like spring, and wipe down those surfaces.

Now that your surfaces are cleared and clean, I'm gonna share my secret to maintaining the surface cleanse, especially on those surfaces that get used constantly. It's called a home base, and you need one for every surface. A home base is a tray or basket or board that practically begs to have stuff put in it or on it. Each often-used surface in my house has one, and I set random things on them during the day so my stuff doesn't clutter up the rest of the cleared-off surface.

In our house, the surface with the highest traffic is our kitchen island. It's ten feet long and constantly holding everything. I came up with a plan to keep it mostly clear and clean so it's always ready to get used up. Yep, that's right, I don't clear my surfaces so they can remain perpetually empty—that's crazy, we live here. I like to keep my surfaces clear so they are always ready to be used for work, dinner, and laundry. Something magical happened when I prioritized a cleared off surface. I found myself naturally cleaning up after myself because the payoff of looking at an empty surface all day was more rewarding than avoiding the ninety second pain of cleaning up. The home base on our kitchen island is a wood board. Yesterday, it had an abandoned snack bag of Cheetos, a stack of receipts, and my empty coffee cup that I planned on using again. Even with all that stuff on the island, the kitchen still felt tidy because all the junk was gathered on home base.

I do the same thing on our all-purpose dining table. Our cat Francie *loves* to sleep on the table, so instead of attempting to retrain Franciecat, I bought a circular basket, and now she has a home base. It's like a cat trap, and she spends about eight hours a day in it.

Give it a try! On each often-used surface, set out some type of home base—a pretty tray, a shallow bowl, a wood box—something that beckons you to set stuff in it so it's not spread out all over the surface. Just watch,

your family will notice and magically set their stuff in the home base too, because it's a stuff magnet.

ADD LIFE WITH PLANTS. When I say plants, I'm referring to potted plants, yard cuttings, and cut flowers. In a perfect world without allergies, I would beg everyone to use real live plants that God created, because there's nothing better. But I totally get that if you or someone in your household has plant allergies, it's probably not worth it to live a life of misery just so you can have real plants in your house. But that is your only out. If you can't have real plants for health reasons, promise me you'll invest in nice pretend plants. Look for plants that aren't too green, because real plants have some yellow and brown undertones. Lots of higher-end stores carry realistic greens. Our patron saint, Joanna Gaines, is a beautiful genius who plants faux plants into planters with real dirt to make them look more authentic! Follow her lead and consider mixing in some faux with live if you need to ease into real plants.

If you are just afraid of using real plants or think it's a waste because they will die, then I want you to step out of your comfort zone and promise yourself you'll at least try real plants—potted plants, yard cuttings, and cut flowers. Here are some tips to help you consider all three.

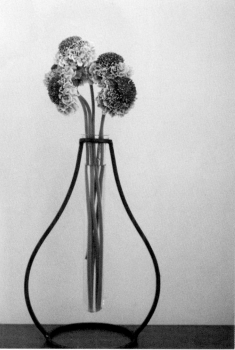

POTTED PLANTS. Guess what, I have killed eighty-five percent of the plants I've purchased in the past ten years. Eventually, every indoor plant I've ever had, or will have, dies. I'm okay with that. But I believe the joy they bring is worth replacing them. If you can keep an eighteen-dollar plant alive for six months, that's three dollars a month or ten cents per day, people. Tell me that's not worth figuring out what kind of plant you can keep alive for years! I've tried following a list of great plants that work for other people, but I've found the best way to find plants that work in my house—with our particular natural lighting setup, and with my personality, meaning I forget to water them unless they are visibly wilting—is to buy a small plant and then just see if I kill it. If I can keep one alive, I buy more! It's fine to have multiples of the same plant in different rooms of your house.

When it comes to the public rooms in your house, aim to have three plants (potted plants, cuttings, or flowers) in every room. If you currently have zero plants, that might sound like a lot, but it will make a huge difference. Start slow, with the goal of one plant per room. Take a few minutes to look at your home boards on Pinterest or flip through your favorite shelter magazine and pay attention to how plants are used in every single room. Think about how the room in each photo would look and feel if the plants weren't there. Rooms without plants often feel drab and sterile. Plants add much-needed life to any room. You deserve life in your home.

Choose a few spots in your house and observe the level of light in those spots. Do these areas get actual sunbeams, which is direct sunlight? Or do they have pretty low and indirect light? Then, off to the home improvement store. There should be a place inside the store (not outside in the nursery) with indoor plants. Every plant should have a tag, and the most important thing you need to look at is what kind of light the plant prefers. Find a plant you like that matches the light you have.

Next, consider the shape of the plant and whether it will be set on the floor, at midlevel on a table, or high up on the top of a bookcase or cupboard. Some plants, such as a fiddle-leaf fig, would look weird sitting up high because you'd be looking at the underside of the leaves. Choose a plant that looks pretty when viewed at the height you need.

Once you have plants, you need planters. Planters are a super fun opportunity to get yourself something to hold your plants that works with your personal style.

Plants and planters are BFFs, and you need both. I mainly stick to white ceramic planters, baskets, and belly bags for texture, and cute bowls and wood planters to add an element of style. After you buy a plant, look for a container a tiny bit larger than the plastic pot the plant comes with. I usually keep the plant in its original pot at least the first few months so I can figure out whether it's the type of plant I won't kill. Simply place the entire plant and its plastic pot into your container.

Bask in the freshness and life that a few little plants add to your space.

The bottom of the plant should be about even with the top of the container. If the plant is too low, raise it up by adding some gravel in the bottom of your container. If your room needs life anyway, go ahead and invest in some great planters that will work with your home year round.

Once you pair those plants with containers (a basket, a little crate, a ceramic planter) and follow the watering directions, bask in the freshness and life that a few little plants add to your space.

YARD CUTTINGS. Yard cuttings are branches, twigs, and shoots you find for free growing outside. Walk around your yard, the abandoned parking lot, your mom's house, your friend's house, and cut off some branches from anything with leaves. Nope, not that short; you need to cut them longer. Go for two to three feet in length. Most cuttings are branches where the beauty climbs all the way up the branch. This is my favorite way to add life to my home, because there's something so right about bringing your local outside in. I would never pull up to a stranger's house and cut stuff, but I have enjoyed a few branches from overgrown bushes in our church parking lot, from the field behind the ice rink, and from a bunch of magnolia trees at a shopping center after a late-season ice storm hit our area and broke them off.

Cuttings are a staple in our house from March through December and are one of the main ways I invite the current season into our home and change it up for free. In the spring, I find that azalea, cherry blossom, Bradford pear, dogwood, lilac, and leafy branches add just the freshness we crave. Plus, it reminds me how much I enjoy cutting things from our yard. I'm no gardener, but I love cutting branches, stems, and flowers so much that every year I add a few more perennial flowers to our yard just so I can cut them and bring them inside next year.

You Need Vases

Most of us don't have a vase to hold even one type of cutting correctly. If you have only that one cut-crystal vase stored under your sink that came with your flowers when you had the baby ten years ago, great, you should keep it. But every home needs a few types of vases.

First consider the vase opening. You'll want vases with openings that are narrow, medium, and wide. Also, to a Cozy Minimalist, vases are an opportunity to add style. You have to use them anyway, why not make a statement? Vases add beauty even when empty. Make sure you have a small collection of vases you like and that work with your decor year round even when empty.

Next, consider vases of different heights: short for the handful of clover your daughter picked at the playground, medium for the grocery store tulips, and tall for the single branch of forsythia blooms.

Personally, I prefer vases that are opaque. Most of the time, I don't want to see the stems of my plants. Your assignment is to shop the house and make sure you have each type of vase in a style you love. If not, instead of buying that cute pink ceramic spring bird, buy yourself the right kinds of vases for your home that you can use year round.

FLOWERS. Whenever I'm hosting, flowers are the gift I give myself. They instantly freshen any room and make a gathering feel special. But when it comes to arranging flowers, many of us are doing it all wrong. We cut our yard cuttings too short and leave our flowers way too long.

Most flowers flower only at the end, so a foot of empty stem isn't all that interesting to look at when it's sitting in your vase. Not only that, but we often set them high up on the mantel so that all we see at eye level is

a bunch of necked stems and the underside of the flowers. Consider the type of flowers you have and whether they'll be best enjoyed looking at them from above, from below, or at eye level, and place them on your surface accordingly.

Most people just cut an inch off the bottom of a bouquet and then put it in the nearest vase. A tall vase is great for long yard cuttings, but usually the worst look for flowers. Clear vases sometimes detract from the flowers themselves because of all those stems. For a bigger impact, cut your flowers shorter and put them in a wider-mouth opaque vase.

I really don't know much about how to arrange flowers, but I have learned what not to do. If I'm at the grocery store, I've found it's better to buy all the same flowers rather than random farm-stand arrangements—it's easier to make lots of the same flower look better. I gravitate toward a round, wide-base vase with a medium opening because the wide roundness helps balance out the flowers. I also love quirky statement vases, such as a vase I have in the shape of a hand, or I sometimes put one of my head-and-bust planters into service as a vase. Also, I've noticed that the flowers have more impact when the blooms start right at the top of each vase, or even hang down to cover some of the vase. You don't want a vase and then twelve inches of stem, and then flowers, so cut your flower stems, and then, probably cut them shorter again.

The Food: Two Foods from Scratch and One Special Drink

If you like the idea of hosting, but the thought of prepping all the food is holding you back, you are going to love how I'm gonna boss you.

I know some folks just love the idea of cooking up a bunch of homemade yums for guests, but our Cozy Minimalist rule for providing food at a gathering is to focus on three things—two foods and one special drink. First, you pick two items to cook or prepare yourself, and the rest is store bought or others brought. This will save you so many times. I *rarely* allow myself to make more than two foods when I'm hosting. You do not need to be glazing the ham, watching over four casseroles, making homemade resurrection rolls, creating three desserts, and prepping countless appetizers. Allow others to help. Allow your favorite restaurant and the grocery store to help too.

Then there is the special drink setup for the occasion. It's true, one of the things people remember from a party are the small details, but I'm not talking about the teeny-tiny handmade paper flowers you spent weeks making for every name tag. While people will notice the details, they won't notice *every* detail. By focusing on a few details and making them extra special, we get to control the details they do remember. Maybe your walls could use a fresh coat of paint, or your patio furniture has seen better days. Guess what, if you provide a few special things to grab people's attention, they won't even notice that stuff. Plus, you're an imperfectionist anyway, so those things will help put people at ease. Focus on providing a unique drink that will take up permanent residence in the memories of your guests.

In the spring, I like to put together an iced-coffee bar. If you're not a fan of coffee, maybe you'll create a signature cocktail, a juice bar, or an infused-water bar. Whatever it is, go the extra mile to put the drink in a beautiful container, provide glass or clear plastic cups, and have something to embellish the drink with, such as fruit, drizzles, toppings, sprinkles, and/or chocolate shavings.

Iced-Coffee Bar

Supplies

- The coffee. This is *the* most important part. You can buy store-bought cold-brew concentrate, you can make a batch of overnight cold brew in your refrigerator (you don't need me to tell you how, just google it), or if you have an espresso machine and are hosting a few friends, you can make two shots of espresso per person. Please note iced coffee is not the same thing as a pot of regular coffee that you let cool off.
- Ice bucket and ice
- Milk and or creamer. I like to provide a few choices like heavy cream, coconut milk, and almond milk.
- Sweetener. Again, if you have lots of guests, it's nice to have a few options like sugar in the raw, Splenda, and honey, or get fancy and make simple syrup.
- Clear glasses
- Straws
- Embellishments like whipped cream, chocolate shavings, and sprinkles if you are feeling extra fancy

I like to make a practice drink before my guests arrive so I can figure out the best ratio and let my guests know what works. Cold brew concentrate and espresso are usually stronger than the overnight cold brew I make at home.

And of course, cute stir sticks, paper straws, chocolate-dipped spoons, or fun drink umbrellas are great for a finishing touch. These are the extra details that make a drink bar so delightful. I like to put everything on a tray in a dedicated area so people can be out of the way putting their drinks together the way they like them. It also acts as an icebreaker, filling what sometimes can be an awkward moment when a new guest arrives by giving them the little task of making themselves a drink. I promise, making one special drink will be more than worth the extra effort.

The People: Your Guests, Yourself, and Your People

The most important part of any gathering is the people. I used to focus on one group of people when it came to hosting—the guests, of course! But there are three people you need to always be mindful of when you are hosting anything at all, and I'm going to remind you of each of them during every season.

The first person to consider are the guests. Regardless of the occasion, think about what you want your guests to experience when they come to your home. I want everyone to feel relaxed and welcomed into a safe and slow place where imperfections are not a surprise, where people are more important than stuff, where there's room and time for them to be heard and to be themselves.

One of the ways we set the tone for real connection is by thinking through the timing of the things that will happen during our gatherings. For example, an arrival time and a starting time.

In spring, we are often hosting birthday parties, showers, and large gatherings, and it's likely that not everyone will know each other. When this is the case, be sure to start the festivities about twenty minutes after the arrival time. It's okay if not every person has arrived. The last time we hosted a huge group, I realized afterward that even though the atmosphere was laid back, we should have started the structured part of our event at the very beginning of the evening, not an hour into the gathering. This structure gives people who don't yet know each other a shared experience that makes it easier for them to connect throughout the rest of the gathering.

Years ago, I went to a wedding shower where I knew only the guest of honor. I arrived at the start time, but the structured part of the party didn't start until more than ninety minutes later. As an introvert, I had what felt like a lifetime of agony making small talk with strangers I'd never see again while I waited for the party to start. Then I had to leave before the gifts

were opened because the gift opening was the last item on the agenda. Be mindful of those who might have a time constraint or might not enjoy an hour of small talk with strangers. Get to the point of the gathering early, and allow the time at the end to be for those who want to linger and engage in conversation.

The next person to be mindful of is you. Before your guests arrive, set aside some time to make sure you are in a hosting mindset. Hosting is about connecting. How do you make sure you're in the right mindset to connect? Embrace the Cozy Minimalist and imperfectionist way. When it comes to setting the mood and the food, you are not going to insist on perfection. You are going to focus on a few important things and make them great, and then you're going to let other things slide.

Give yourself grace and ample time to prepare, and decide in advance to allow for imperfections.

Next, you need to be mindful of the others in your household. Just giving them a simple reminder of what's happening and when and of any expectations you have of them can make a world of difference.

BEAUTIFULLY IMPERFECT

As you focus on the mood, the food, and the people, you can let everything else go and still have a memorable, meaningful gathering for you, your family, and your guests.

When it comes to spring hosting, once you springify your home, all you need to do to get your home ready for guests is to simplify and add life. Start with a surface cleanse to remove those accumulated layers of stuff, designate a home base on each surface, and then add life with plants.

Your goal is to implement the rule of three by adding three plants with containers to your home, making three foods (two from scratch and one special drink), and considering the three people at every gathering.

There's no need to turn into a crazy person scrubbing the wall behind the fridge, re-landscaping the back yard, and getting a spray tan before you invite people over.

You can trust in the people-easing power of imperfections. You can give yourself grace and plan for and allow your life and home to be seen for what they really are: a beautiful mess. Sharing some of your everyday imperfectness is the main ingredient needed to connect with people. Trying to finish every project, redecorate every room, overthink, or overspend takes away from your goal. It's your job not to do that. People remember being loved, welcomed, included, and heard. They don't remember whether your china cabinet was dust free.

This spring, welcome people into your lived-in and loved-on home in the midst of your beautiful mess.

SUMMER

CHAPTER 7

SUMMER SEASON

Thou Burning Sun with
Golden Beam

There is such a thing
as sacred idleness.

—George Macdonald, *Lilith*

In the early years of my design work, a client invited me to help her with her home. More than anything, she wanted to incorporate elements of her favorite place in the world—the beach—into her landlocked home in the piedmont of North Carolina. She told me her plans of placing on various out-of-the-way surfaces around her house buckets of sand and shells to get that beachy feel she craved. I'll wait while you go back and read that sentence again.

I love that this woman had a place in the world that felt so welcoming to her that she wanted to incorporate it into her home. I think we can all relate to wanting the place where we feel most alive to be represented in the place where we spend most of our time. I completely agree that a sandy beach with gentle waves, swaying palm trees, and a constant warm breeze is one of the most relaxing places in the world. I think the universal logo for relaxation is two palm trees on a deserted beach with a hammock tied between. You know the one. The problem, in this case, was in being too literal.

I'm guessing the reason my client loved the beach had less to do with the sand and more to do with the feeling of peace, serenity, and closeness to creation and God that she experienced when she was there. I'm sure the fact that she was on vacation also contributed to the feelings of freedom, wholeness, and purpose she felt there. Often when we take time away from the stresses of life and spend time enjoying our family and creation, we equate those happy feelings with the place where we experience them.

I'm not here to ask existential questions such as, Which came first, relaxation or the beach? But I have wondered, do we identify swaying palms with relaxation because we experience them while we are on vacation, or are they inherently relaxing, so we gravitate to them when we have a break? The truth is, it doesn't matter which leads to what. But as a person who has lived at the beach,

I can attest to the fact that it loses a bit of its luster when you are living your nine-to-five life cooking dinner and doing laundry two miles away from the shoreline.

A large part of the reason we enjoy being at the beach—or wherever it is we spend our vacations—is that we are purposeful about relaxing and enjoying life. We create space to relax, therefore we are relaxed. As crazy as it was to think that sprinkling actual sand around her actual house would help her experience those beachy vibes and a more relaxed life, there is some truth behind what this well-meaning beach mom was trying to do. You and I can have a summer house, and we don't have to buy a vacation home or bags of playground sand to get it.

CONSUMER SUMMER VERSUS CREATOR SUMMER

How we go about creating our summer homes can have a huge impact on how we feel about them and on how much time and money they require. Let's explore the two mindsets we get to choose between as we set up our summer homes. In the past, I thought my only choice was to have a consumer summer home full of summer visuals so everyone would know how much I love summer. Now I realize I have a choice, and so do you. We don't have to have a consumer summer. We can choose to honor summer like our Creator.

Consumer Summer

I told that story of the beach-loving, sand-spreading client with a chuckle, but the truth is, for years, my own summer decor followed the same sentiment. It just wasn't quite as tricky to clean up. Every summer I'd find myself considering huge paintings of waves, wondering if I made the wrong choice when I bought a dark leather sofa and wishing I could lighten and brighten up every room of my house.

But I couldn't afford to buy huge, three-month-use paintings or a new sofa. And the only way I knew to lighten and brighten up what I had was to buy a bunch of light colored, summery items and add them to my already full house. I longed for my home to feel like a respite during a hot summer day.

I wanted it to be simple but pretty, and for the life of me, I had no idea how to accomplish that. So I listened to the stores and believed that I must not have had enough of the right stuff. I had a cute collection of summer decor that I brought out every summer, but secretly I wondered why it made my house feel heavier and more complicated.

If you can relate to any of these feelings, you might be trapped by the idea that a consumer summer is the only option. I'm happy to report there is another way.

Creator Summer

As Cozy Minimalists, we are beauty hunters who look to creation for our cues each season as we refresh the look of our homes. When I think about how I really experience summer in nature, it's all about warmth, light, sky, clouds, leafy trees, Queen Anne's lace, fireflies, and large bodies of cool, refreshing water. When I gather inspiration photos that represent summer to me, they center around the colors blue and green, and images of water, sky, green fields, and leafy trees.

When I think about how I really experience summer in nature, it's all about warmth, light, sky, clouds, leafy trees, Queen Anne's lace, fireflies, and large bodies of cool, refreshing water.

By now, you probably know that the secret to seasonalizing your home without filling it with store-bought decor is to cater to all five senses. In this chapter, we're going to devote more attention to indoor spaces, and in the next chapter, we'll focus on creating a summer vibe in outdoor spaces.

As it is with every season, your home assignment begins with collecting images for inspiration. Lucky you, this is so fun! The only difference this time is that I want you to collect both outdoor images of creation that feel like summer to you, and indoor photos of homes that are unmistakably summer in all the best ways. Collecting images of summery homes you are drawn to will help you pay attention to what communicates summer to you, and what you, in turn, want to share with everyone who enters your home this season.

When you see a home, a room, a patio, or anything else on Instagram or Pinterest that feels like summer to you, save it in an album or folder. Once you have a good collection, look through those photos and ask yourself what they have in common. This is always the first step to seasonalizing your home. Now focus on the feeling the photos evoke in you. For you, maybe summer is about wonder and peace, travel, recreation, adventure, and freedom. If so, making your home feel like summer might mean clearing out some space by removing stressful distractions like the stack of papers that you need to file, the exercise equipment you keep meaning to post on Craigslist, and the winter clothes that have been piling up in the corner of your bedroom. If your summer ideal is rich with images of abundance, verdant fields, and hydrangeas bending under the weight of their blooms, then frequent visits to the farmers market or starting a flower garden may be priorities for you this summer.

If I'm at a loss and need inspiration for creating a seasonal feeling in my home, I turn to my inspiration photos and remind myself of what feels like summer to me. My photos are an instant giveaway that during summer, I long for white space, green leaves, natural light, woven baskets, hats and

Spring into Summer

Although I believe we should give ourselves the gift of slow transitions between seasons in our homes, the start of a new season is always a good reminder to take a quick walk through the house looking for seasonal items that I no longer need.

Now is the time pack up any lingering winter-into-spring throws, pillows, and bedding.

The pools are open and if your family is frequenting pools like we are, you might want to pack away some jackets, raincoats, and rainboots to create a place to stash the lunch cooler and hang beach towels and the beach bag.

If you have any plants that prefer to summer on the porch, now's the time to move them outside for a few months. I love my fiddle-leaf fig trees, and they look great in my house, but I put them on our covered porch every summer and they reward me by growing like crazy.

Walk around your house to see if you can pack away anything you won't be needing for the summer.

wicker, blues and greens. Then I keep all that in mind as I make summer decor decisions in my home.

So go ahead and collect some images—both outdoor and indoor—and then work through each of the five senses to bring what you love most about summer into your home. When you embrace summer through the five senses, anyone who enters your home will be able to tell what season it is without being reminded by a machine-lettered "On Lake Time" wooden sign. And there's the bonus that your home will automatically be ready for hosting everything from Memorial Day to Labor Day, including graduation parties, Fourth of July, and impromptu s'mores nights.

THE FIVE SENSES OF SUMMER

Now for the fun part! Even if summer isn't your favorite season, after collecting summer inspiration images, you've now done a little homework to remind yourself of your favorite parts of the season. You get to apply everything you love about summer into your home simply by working through the five senses.

Sight: The Look of Summer

A few times in my life, I've been lucky enough to stay in or visit the kind of summer vacation home that felt just right. These places were similar to those beach houses featured in movies and described in our favorite beach reads. I've figured out what these dreamy, restful spaces have in common so I can bring that feeling to my everyday house. These beachy vacation homes are always cool, calm, and collected.

COOL. In the summer, we don't want our houses to be too hot physically or to look too hot visually. The simplest way to visually cool down your home is by adding some cool colors like blues and greens. The color white can have the same power as a cool color too. It can instantly neutralize, quiet, and lighten whatever color it's paired with, so include it on your cool list. You can add some cool colors, including whites, no matter what the main colors are in your home.

Most of my big decor is season neutral, but I have a few pieces that feel like they relate to one season more than others. I make sure those pieces are front and center during the season they seem to promote. In summer, I emphasize cool by setting my big blue Dutch oven on the stove and keeping my blue ceramic urn stocked with anything that's green, leafy, or blooming, even if it's just a few tree branches. Shop your house for items in the cool colors you love, and place them front and center.

Speaking of color, summer is a great time to take a little risk and add some low-commitment color to your home. If your leather sofa is feeling heavy and wintery, that doesn't mean you should buy a sky-blue sofa so it will feel summery; it means you might add some pillows in cool, summery colors. If your room doesn't have much white, maybe you can simply lighten and neutralize that wintery-feeling sofa by adding a few large white pillows. I think

Calm

Four Summer Tips Especially for Moms

1. **ADD A SUMMER SURFACE.** We bought it in the fall and called it the homework table, but it got just as much attention during the summer months. I spent seventy dollars for a small breakfast table from Kmart and pushed it against the window at the end of the family room. Voila! Instant summer surface for puzzles, crafts, or coloring.

2. **STRIP THE FRIDGE.** The fridge is the kitchen equivalent of the bottom of your purse—it's where all the bits and pieces collect. Just because someone invited you to it, announced it, sent you a photo of it, or drew it doesn't mean it has to live on your refrigerator until the Second Coming.

   Summer is a great time to strip down the fridge and let it run around naked for a while. Surprisingly, a naked fridge has a calming effect in the kitchen. Go ahead and try it right now. Enter any major dates into your calendar, keep any major announcements in a basket or drawer, and clear off that fridge.

3. **CREATE CUP CENTRAL.** Every summer, about two weeks after our three boys were home, I'd start to wonder why my sink was full of used cups and glasses. It turns out each cup was used for two sips of lemonade, then thrown in the sink. Forty-five minutes later, the same thing happened again with a fresh cup, all day, every day, times three boys. To stop the madness, I bought glasses in different styles that I loved, one style for each boy, and two glasses in that style per boy. I set out a pretty wooden dish rack on a pretty dish towel next to the sink. I let the boys know which style belonged to them and that these were the only glasses they were allowed to use. They could rinse out their cups and let them hang out on the dish rack until they got thirsty again. This solved all of our problems and made me suddenly rich and thin. Or at least it helped with the sink-o-cups issue.

4. **CONSIDER GOING RUGLESS FOR SUMMER.** If you have a lot of large or heavy rugs, good for you! So many people underestimate the power of the right-sized rug. However, come summer, your home can begin to feel heavy, and one easy way to lighten it up is to roll up the rugs for a season. I usually remove the rug under our dining area, and one year I never put it back. It's still not there.

every summer room can benefit from a touch of white. A new sofa is a big commitment; a new pillow is a small one. Take inventory of your room, noting both the color and texture of the fabrics of your rugs, drapes, pillows, throws, and bedding. Consider trading out anything overly heavy for something lighter in both color and fabric. These small changes can really make a big impact in lightening up your home for summer.

COLLECTED. Collections make a big impact when they're displayed. I keep my straw hats hanging on the back-porch wall all year round. They are in the perfect spot for me to grab one before I head out to the pool or to weed the flower bed. But even when they aren't doing their job shielding me from the sun, they look fantastic grouped together on the wall.

> If you want your collectables to have the visual impact they deserve, group them and they'll make one large power statement.

I have a small collection of green glass vases I store out in our barn, but come summer, I move them to our patio so they can get extra attention. If you want your collectables to have the visual impact they deserve, group them and they'll make one large power statement. Whatever it is that you collect—globes, photos in silver frames, maps, blue-and-white china—group it all together. Cool, calm, and collected leads to a simple, summer-feeling home.

Touch: The Feel of Summer

In the summer, I focus on the fabrics in our home. I don't want to be surrounded by materials that feel hot to the touch or even look hot. Our family room has blue as a main accent color, so I use blue year round. The seasons don't boss my house and my favorite colors. But in some seasons, I'm drawn to richer colors and warm off-whites, furs, and textures. Together, these items feel warm and comforting, heavy and wintery. I keep my blue pillows out year round, but in summer I want a more playful feel with lightweight stripes, whites, and, depending on my mood, crisp blacks and whites. My pillow-family colors and fabrics transition just as the seasons do.

Recreation versus Amusement

More than any other season, summer for our family is about rest and recreation while enjoying creation. The word *recreation* literally means "to be re-created." Recreational activities are things we do that are life-giving, such as sitting next to a stream, hiking through an open field, watching the night sky for stars. If you are more outdoorsy than me, it may be that activities such as whitewater rafting, mountain biking, and camping are recreational for you.

In contrast, amusement is all about diverting and holding our attention. In her book *Choosing Rest,* Sally Breedlove says *amusement* literally means "to not think." There's a time and a place for amusement (hello Netflix), but if our lives consist only of work or being amused, it won't be long until we begin to feel that something is missing.

When our boys were young teenagers, we were given a trip to Disney World. It was fun, but by the end of it, we were all left with an empty, zombie-like feeling. That, in a nutshell, is the aftermath of amusement. I think the boys were the ones who noticed it the most. They didn't even want to go to the parks the last day we were there, opting to have a slow day around the hotel swimming and walking the nature paths. After that trip, we decided that our family trips would include mostly restorative, recreational time with a tiny bit of amusement thrown in. It's made all the difference in our vacations. Sometimes we come home exhausted, but it's a restorative tired, not a blank-stare tired.

I think the benefits of recreation motivate us to bring elements from our favorite vacation spots into our homes. Because at the beach, or wherever we go on vacation, we experience recreation. But instead of focusing on the decor to make our houses look like our vacation spots, we need to focus on creating an atmosphere or environment at home that allows us to experience true recreation.

In his book *Atomic Habits,* James Clear writes, "Environment is the invisible hand that shapes human behavior." We can nudge people to take action just by what we put in front of them. Basically, we can commit mind control with decorating. Well, almost.

If your goal is to foster recreational and restorative activities at home, then create spaces that readily invite people to take action—or nonaction. This kind of purposeful placemaking makes a huge impact on how we experience a space. Yes, a summery vignette on a mantel can be pretty, but a home put together with rest and recreation in mind actually does shape human behavior.

Here are a few tips to help you create a recreational summery home.

- Create a reading nook by providing comfy seating, a reading light, and of course great books, magazines, and coloring books for all ages.
- Create a dedicated space for napping outdoors. When is the last time you took a nap outside? Outside naps are one of the most magical experiences of summer, and every house should have at least one place where a person could take a nap outside. A hammock, outdoor chaise lounge, or even a quilt and a pillow under a shade tree will be a welcome addition to any home.
- Provide a big empty surface in a public room for a life-giving project. A stack of puzzles, a basket of Legos, board games, or a simple craft all deserve to be out in the open, especially in the summer. Keep whatever it is at the ready as an invitation to rest and recreate.

I crave a lightened up look for my dark sofa in the summer, so I make sure some of my largest pillows are lighter in color and fabric. Notice all the different sizes of pillows. Most of us make the mistake of using pillows that are too small. The anchor pillows in each corner of a sofa should be at least twenty-four inches across.

I didn't buy any new pillow covers in the spring, just switched out pillow covers. But this year, my old summer pillows and throws felt tired, so I found a few new pillows (feather stuffed with covers that zip off so I can wash them) and a few throws in summery colors. It's still important to have texture in the summer so that our rooms have some roughage to stop the eye. Otherwise, the room "runs," and who wants to hang out in a room that feels like it has diarrhea? High-texture items such as baskets, wicker, and wood, when balanced with white, look so summery and beachy. This doesn't mean you have to trade out everything you own for lightweight materials. But just by switching out a heavy planter for a basket, you can make your home feel like it recognizes and is in tune with the season.

In the fall and winter, I tend to use neutral, patterned sheets and mix them all up for fun. But by summer, I want our bed to feel like a cool and welcome oasis rather than a den for an arctic sleep. Switching to all-white sheets and linens in the spring and summer makes the room feel lighter, and the bed reads as a cool, welcoming, nappable retreat. I also take the top blanket off the bed and remove the fussy decorative pillows—simplicity feels like luxury in the summer. Come fall, I'll be ready for my textured pillows and blanket again.

Hearing: The Sound of Summer

When I was growing up in southern Indiana, it was summer more than any other season that had its own soundtrack. The night air was filled with the sounds of cicadas, katydids, and crickets. Morning, of course, was for the mourning doves. One of my favorite summer songs, which brings tears to my eyes when I hear it, starts with the sound of children splashing in water and laughing in the background. Whatever sounds like summer to you, make it a point to put yourself in the way of summer sounds. That doesn't mean buying a CD of crickets. Nope, y'all, we are not doing that. Usually, when I'm longing

for summer sounds, it means I need to spend some time sitting on the porch when the crickets are chirping.

Make your own summer playlist and play it over the summer during gatherings, while you're cooking dinner, or driving to the Fourth of July barbecue at your sister's house. Then, once fall comes, don't listen to the summer list again. Next year, when you play your summer list for the first time, something magical will happen: the songs and sounds you curated will *feel* like summer no matter where you are or what you are doing.

Smell: The Scent of Summer

What smells like summer to you? Maybe it's charcoal, fresh-cut grass, citronella candles, coconut-scented sunscreen, a special blend of essential oils, or basil dish soap. Don't neglect your sense of smell this summer. Bring all the summery scents into your home by buying the sunscreen, soap, and foods that smell like summer to you.

Cut some honeysuckle and bring it into the house or grab a bouquet of peonies at the farmers market and take a whiff every time you walk by.

Sit outside and breathe deeply when the neighbors cut the grass. Light that summer-scented candle you bought last year. Candles around the world are sitting in drawers hoping to one day be dusted off and actually lit. Make your candle's dream come true and light it today.

Taste: The Flavor of Summer

Summer tastes like watermelon, just about anything grilled, salads, tomatoes, cucumbers, corn on the cob, lemonade, strawberries, fresh basil, peaches, and blueberries. Oh my gosh, summer is so good to us! Part of getting your home ready for summer is the joy of providing some summer foods for your family. Get the supplies you need for the grill, such as charcoal or propane. Clear out space in the freezer for those mini ice cream cones, extra popsicles, and frozen burgers you can have on hand just in case. And don't forget to stock up on s'mores supplies, even if you have to make them in the microwave. Pick up an herb plant early in the season so you can add your own basil to a plate of farmers market tomatoes, or enjoy a garnish of fresh mint with your summer lemonade. You will feel like a fancy farmer with your homegrown salads and minty drinks.

Having a summer home and summer supplies is so much more fun and delicious than just setting out some pretend shell decor. Give yourself credit and a high five for welcoming summer through the foods you eat. Your entire family will rise up and call you blessed.

SUMMER SUPPLIES

Instead of stocking your home with store-bought summer decor, stock it with summer supplies. Crisp white sheets, summer colors, lightweight throws, leafy branches, fresh fruit, lighthearted music, simple snacks. Think about it—once you make your home cooler, calmer, and a tiny bit more collected, it will undeniably feel like summer. Everyone in your household will appreciate the different ways you welcome the season into your home. Visual decor is nice, but supplies that cater to the five senses are unforgettable.

Here are a few items to consider:

- Glasses suitable for fun, fruity drinks
- Picnic containers, such as a cooler or a basket
- Sticks for cooking hot dogs or marshmallows over an open fire
- An extra quilt or blanket for the trunk of the car, just in case you can stop for that impromptu picnic
- A big fruit bowl to hold seasonal fruit on your kitchen counter
- White sheets, white duvet cover, white towels to neutralize and brighten
- A summer playlist

When you have seasonal supplies at your fingertips, you'll always be ready to create simple, impromptu experiences centered around eating summery foods, taking time to relax (even if for only a few minutes), and enjoying your simplified home.

Paying attention to creation and what you enjoy about summer is the ideal place to start before you make any purchases to summerize your home. I hope this method becomes second nature for you like it has for me. Now, welcoming each season into your home will feel like a natural response to what is happening outside your four walls.

In creation, moving from season to season is never an abrupt change, and it doesn't have to be in your home. No longer will you have to block out a Saturday to pack away a bunch of spring decor only to add a new layer of summer decor. Or if you never did that, at least now you know that's not the only way to create a summer home. Now you can slowly add some summer to your spring by switching out any low-commitment hot colors for cooler colors, adding a sense of calm to your home by removing some things, and making sure your collections are one big happy family. Of course, you'll still buy things, but isn't it better to purchase items you can use for longer than a season? This is how we welcome the season into our homes as Cozy Minimalists. And the best part is, once you summerize your home, you'll practically be ready to host.

Once you make your home cooler, calmer, and a tiny bit more collected, it will undeniably feel like summer.

CHAPTER 8

SUMMER CELEBRATION

All the Earth Shall Praise Thy
Name in Earth and Sky and Sea

> Our theology is best
> expressed in our hospitality.
>
> —Ann Voskamp

For the first time in our twenty-five years of marriage and living in fourteen different houses, our back yard is the nicest room in our house. I want *you* to know that *I* know we do not have a typical back yard. We bought this fixer-upper seven years ago with purpose. The property had a house we could live in and a barn we wanted to use for gatherings. We bought it with guests in mind. I was confident I could make any house look my style, so when we property shopped, our focus was all about what the property offered for gathering spaces. We knew this place needed a ton of work, but we also knew it would be worth it.

One item on our ton-of-work-to-do list was the built-in, twenty-five-year-old vinyl pool with a broken main drain. We were committed to redoing the old pool, and we hoped that one day we'd be able to make the back yard into our dream-come-true outdoor room. It didn't hurt that Chad had been working for one of his closest friends, a commercial pool builder. Chad, his friends, and our boys built our entire back yard. They enjoyed the process so much that Chad and his friend ended up starting their own business building residential pools. So in addition to looking at these photos and seeing a fun back yard, I hope you also see our heart behind it, which is a commitment to gathering people.

Our house is right at two thousand square feet, but this yard makes our house seem huge. Plus, we live in North Carolina, so we get to be outside and use it year round. I am out here almost daily. I've had twenty-five years of experience creating and using outdoor spaces in every possible scenario, from living in rental houses to living in a condo neighborhood of elderly folks (with our three rowdy boys), from having new-subdivision back yards with zero trees to having yards so small they were practically laughable.

All of which is to say that after moving fourteen times and living in all different kinds of houses, we've experienced just about every type of backyard situation there is and still found a way to use each one to host guests outside. Every yard had some redeeming quality, and I promise that your yard has a redeeming quality too. Even if you have to borrow a patch of grass from the park down the street, you'll get the redeeming quality of not having to mow it. Every scenario has a win.

We didn't wait until we had a finished back yard to host outdoor gatherings. We've been inviting people over in the midst of every situation our entire marriage, and we've had just as much fun circled around a bonfire sitting on stumps as we've had playing volleyball in the pool.

If you've read this book through each season, you've probably picked up on the rhythm of how to approach every gathering. No matter the gathering or celebration, if you've already seasonalized your home, you can trust the process and focus on just three things: the mood, the food, and the people. This, of course, applies to summer gatherings too. But because summer is a season of relaxed casualness and because I know how daunting it can be to invite people over no matter the season, for summer, we're gonna shake things up a bit.

If you need a baby step to finally invite the neighbors over, or if you have a full summer and hosting feels like it could get lost in the shuffle, I think you'll love the doable ideas in this chapter. I've found it's a million times easier to invite people over when the gathering takes place outside. And I don't want you to finish this book without putting its ideas into action and opening up your home, or in this case your yard.

Whether you have a tiny deck, a side porch, or a grassy area under a tree, are borrowing the park picnic tables, or have acres of space, there are a few things to keep in mind that will help you create your own outdoor room as the backdrop for summer memories you'll hold dear for years.

We didn't wait until we had a finished back yard to host outdoor gatherings. We've had just as much fun circled around a bonfire sitting on stumps as we've had playing volleyball in the pool.

DECORATING YOUR OUTDOOR SPACE

The whole point of being outside is to enjoy the outdoors, to let heaven and nature sing. We don't need to add to the beauty God has already provided by piling on a bunch of store-bought stuff. As with every other season, you'll choose a few things to focus on, and then you can forget the rest.

Before you start buying the same outdoor furniture your favorite Instagrammer has, you need to know the difference between creating uncovered and covered outdoor spaces.

Uncovered versus Covered Outdoor Spaces

Is your outdoor area roofed or roofless? As Cozy Minimalists, we approach these two spaces very differently. We can't compare our uncovered space to someone's covered space; they are two very different things.

UNCOVERED OUTDOOR SPACES. Uncovered areas are wonderful because you can have real fires, see the stars at night, and feel like you are really outside—because you are! If you have an uncovered outdoor area, congratulations! You have a wonderful outdoor room.

The primary thing you need to decide before you buy anything is what level of care you are willing to devote to the things you want to use in your outdoor space. Are you the kind of person who doesn't mind protecting cushions and pillows by storing them away or covering them every time you are done using your outdoor space? Or do you already know that once you set up your room, you don't want to devote any time to keeping up with it?

When it comes to uncovered outdoor spaces, I'm what my friend Kendra calls a lazy genius. Not only do I want the most style with the least amount of stuff, but as a lazy genius, I want the best look with the least amount of upkeep.

The goal for my uncovered space is that everything from the outdoor furniture to the decor to the lighting be able to sit outside no matter what the weather. I need my outdoor furniture to live its best life without depending on me to run the cushions in every time there's a dark cloud. That means I have to be pickier about what I choose to use in my uncovered space, because some types of items will fall apart or straight-up look awful after sitting in the weather for even a week. But I'm good with that. I've decided the trade-offs—doing a big cleaning once a year and not spending any time in my life looking after my stuff—are worth it.

Patio Arrangement Tips

1. **USE FURNITURE THAT CONTRASTS WITH YOUR BACKGROUND.**
   We have an uncovered outdoor eating area. There's an umbrella off to
   the side for shade, but this part of the patio gets natural shade in the
   afternoon and evening. When we first got our wood table, I placed it in
   the middle of the patio, but it was visually lost without any contrast with
   the background. But doesn't it look really nice against a white wall?

   If you have white furniture outside, try to place it in front of a dark or
   woodsy/treed/gardeny background. If you have wood or dark furniture,
   it will pop and look extra pretty against a light background.

2. **CREATE ZONES.** My back patio is laid out in zones. It's not one huge
   pile of furniture. We have an eating zone, an outdoor fireplace zone
   where the cushions can get rained on, and a covered zone with white
   cushions that need a little more babying. Just as you have certain areas
   for certain things inside your home, create zones to help spread the love
   in your yard or on your porch or patio.

3. **PLACE CHAIRS IN PAIRS.** Purchase and place your chairs in pairs.
   This tip applies to indoor and outdoor rooms. Place pairs of chairs off
   by themselves and tucked away in corners to foster good conversation,
   whether the gathering is huge or tiny.

Decide now how attentive you want to be to your uncovered room.

Low-maintenance function and beauty is my goal with a roofless room.
I don't have time to pamper outdoor rugs, lamps, feather pillows, and stuff
that could blow away or get moldy. I *never* use outdoor rugs in an uncovered
space; they always end up looking like they need to be vacuumed all of the
time. No thanks, I'm already feeling bad enough about not vacuuming my
indoor rugs.

I use the same low-maintenance approach for cushions. The only time I remove the cushions in my uncovered space is if we're hosting a party tomorrow and it's going to rain today. Our cushions will eventually mildew, but pressure-washing them once a year brings them back to life. They are high-quality outdoor cushions that are somewhat lightweight, and the water seems to drain right out of them.

If you have outdoor cushions you want to leave out, you'll need to learn how much time it takes for your cushions to dry, and then you can create your own rule for whether you need to protect them from rain before you host something. Personally, I'd rather pressure-wash the cushions once a year than treat them like queens that have to be tucked in every night. You get to make your own decision about cushion care. It's all about trade-offs. If you are a person who will cover your cushions or pack them away after each use, I applaud you! I just know that won't work for me.

The truth is, there is no fabric that can sit out in the weather and last forever. Yes, you can buy fabric sealant and spray it on your cushions, and you should. But just as there is no sofa you can buy for your home that will look like new after ten years of using it, your patio furniture will eventually become worn. My furniture is there to serve me. I don't want to destroy it, but I'm not going to make choices that set me up to babysit diva furniture. I'd rather it rot than boss me around. I am the boss of my cushions; you are the boss of yours.

Here are your options when it comes to outdoor cushions.

- Don't put fabric cushions outside, especially uncovered.
- Set out fabricy things only when you are going to use them, then store them immediately when you are done.
- Buy patio covers for everything and keep fabrics covered when not in use.
- Choose the best possible fabric/cushion option and coat them with spray-on fabric sealant. Pressure-wash them once a year and know that one day you'll have to replace them.
- Choose the least expensive fabric option knowing that you'll just buy new stuff next year.

A Cozy Minimalist creates a space
that is inviting all day, every day,
not one she has to rush to put
together in time for visitors.

You want to create a place that will look good even if it's not freshly pressure-washed and swept so that you don't hate seeing it and feel guilty on a daily basis. Most likely, you and your family will be looking at your patio area all the time. A Cozy Minimalist creates a space that is inviting all day, every day, not one she has to rush to put together in time for visitors. For me, I'm really happy with how our patio looks no matter the weather. Plus, we live in a climate where we use our outdoor rooms year round.

COVERED OUTDOOR SPACES. Covered areas are wonderful because they offer some shelter from the weather for both people and things. You can enjoy sitting outside during a thunderstorm or plan an outdoor gathering without having a contingency plan in case it rains. Covered areas give you an opportunity to use all sorts of stuff you wouldn't want to use if it were exposed to the weather. That means you have a lot more options when it comes to decorating a covered area, but you do lose a bit of that expansive outdoor feeling. It's a trade-off.

Since our covered area is so well protected, I opted for white sofa cushions. We still pressure-wash the cushions once a year, but they are slower to mildew because they have a roof over their heads. A rule of thumb: you can use light cushions outdoors under a roof, and darker cushions are usually best out in the open.

Your goal is to choose the right cushion for the space and for your personality.

With a covered area, you can use almost anything as long as it won't be bothered by humidity and temperature changes. Keep in mind that on stormy days, you might get a little rain coming in, and that just as it is with indoor items, anything directly in sunlight might fade over time. But for the most part, even indoor wood furniture can last for years when protected in a covered outdoor area.

Lighting

Outdoor lighting makes a nighttime gathering magical. If you want to up the cozy factor, add fire. Whether you use candles, a bonfire, tiki torches, a fireplace, or a firepit, fire is a must-have for any nighttime gathering.

Just as it is with furniture and cushions, lighting options are different for covered and uncovered spaces. Someone recently asked me if the lamp on our covered porch is an outdoor lamp. It's not, and I also didn't realize there was such a thing as an outdoor lamp. Even though it's well protected, I know I might need to replace the shade one day. And I'm good with that.

In both covered and uncovered spaces, outdoor strings of lights are one of my favorite ways to light up an area. When we moved to this property, the first thing I bought was a set of heavy-duty outdoor string lights. They cost just forty-nine dollars, and they've been going strong for six years. It's worth the extra effort to secure them permanently because these string lights will last for years through all sorts of weather. We never take ours down, just replace bulbs when they burn out.

Plants

I've learned that it's easier to keep potted plants alive in the covered areas, so in uncovered areas, I rely mostly on plants planted in the ground. I stay away from anything in pots unless it's a special occasion or I've recently recommitted my life to watering outdoor plants. Plants in pots and exposed to the sun need to be watered much more often than plants in the ground.

By being mindful about the kind of outdoor space you have and the amount of upkeep you're willing to put up with, you will be able to make informed decisions about what types of seating and surfaces are the best fit for your outdoor area. Adding a sprinkling of low maintenance plants and some lighting for ambiance sets the mood for cozy connection.

SIMPLE HOSPITALITY

Some of the fondest memories I have are from the days when we lived in neighborhoods where the houses were built impossibly close together. We'd be outside and see a neighbor over the fence, and within a few minutes they'd walk through the side gate of our back yard to hang out. We'd be barefoot, they'd bring their own drinks, and the kids would turn up in bathing suits, princess costumes, or robes from tae kwon do practice. The memories are great because this happened often and it was true connection, nothing fancy about it. These low-key gatherings were always easy, organic, and a hundred percent stress free.

How can we foster such low-stress, high-connection time with friends? By recreating that easy, organic, stress-free atmosphere. These times together were unplanned and spur of the moment, which meant there were zero expectations and zero worries for me as a host. We just wanted to hang out.

You can do this.

A Last-Minute Invitation

Your mission is to invite someone for a spur-of-the-moment outdoor hangout at your house. It might be a couple, a family, a neighbor, or the fun single parent from carpool. Some of us are out of practice and need a little kickstart to hospitality, and summer is the *perfect* time for that. Summer is a time of low expectations, and once you get your outdoor space ready, all you have to do is clean one toilet—in case anyone needs to go to the bathroom—and you are done. And if you don't have any outdoor space in your life right now, borrow some and host your impromptu meet-up at a park.

The goal is to set expectations low by inviting your guests at the last minute. If you need to secretly make a few simple plans in your head so you can feel like a person and not panic, that's fine. Then call, text, or Facebook your nearby friends *only* a few hours before you want them to show up. And have a list of three to five friends you can do this with, because there's a good chance the first people you call can't come. That's normal because this is last minute. No worries, we have low expectations. We just want to hang out.

Tell your friends that you know it's last minute, but you'd love to see them and want to know if they want to come hang out in the back yard, on the porch, around the firepit, at the park, or wherever you want to hang out. Make sure you mention they'll be outside so they can dress accordingly. You are going to be so good at this! Plus, this simple hosting style is going to remind you of how enjoyable it is to have people over because all it requires

is an outdoor space and a few other things. We'll get to those in just a second. The best part of this sneaky unplan is that your guests already know to expect crazy casual since this was a last-minute invite. They'll feel special that you just want to spend time with them. No one expects a four-course meal, a flower arrangement, or toys off the floor; it's all about connecting. No one has to know what all the rooms in your house look or even smell like. Plus, simple, easy-to-implement plans mean you are going to follow through with the impromptu invite.

Here are just a few things to keep in mind to provide for your guests.

Seating, Surfaces, and Comfort

Seating and surfaces can be as simple as quilts and pillows placed on the ground, and trays or wood stumps work great as surfaces for food and drinks. The bare minimum of a place to sit your heinie and a place to set your drink feels inviting and purposeful simply because you thought ahead and provided them.

We have some of those plastic, twenty-dollar Adirondack chairs from the grocery store that have served us well for seating. They are one step above the quilt if you want something to get you and your guests off the ground. But don't get hung up on whether to provide chairs. Remember, the goal is to remove any and all excuses to wait to invite people over. I promise, you already have something you can use for people to sit on outside; it doesn't have to be the latest outdoor furniture set with matching umbrellas and pillows.

As far as comfort goes, if it's going to be hot and sunny when your guests are there, provide shade—either natural shade in the form of trees, or store-bought shade in the form of umbrellas or sun shades or a covered patio. If you don't have any shade, plan to gather near sunset so the glaring hot sun doesn't make you and your guests want to run indoors for the air-conditioning.

I've heard wild rumors of places that get cold at night in the summer. If you live in one of those exotic locales, be sure to provide some way for your guests to stay warm. Throws and blankets or a fire are simple options. If there's a chance of rain, have a covered place or be okay with guests coming inside. And if it's buggy, be sure to have a citronella candle or even smoke from your fire or tiki torches.

Impromptu Provisions

Even though this is last minute, you'll want to have a few essentials on hand for last-minute invitations. This is where your summer-supply-gathering mindset really pays off. You can pick up a few things at the beginning of the season so you'll always be ready for a casual invite.

EDIBLES. For your last-minute gathering, provide only two edibles: one drink and one food. That's all you need. If you plan a fancy presentation, your guests will think you have some other friends who canceled at the last minute and they are the replacements. Do not offend your friends by being too elaborate. Keep it simple.

Your drink could be lemonade, sangria, or a cooler filled with bottled drinks. If you want to feel fancy but not be fancy, make two-ingredient prosecco pops for the adults. Simply unwrap a fruity popsicle, put it stick up in a wine glass, and fill the glass with prosecco. Be sure to wait until your guests arrive and pour it right in front of them for the full effect. Prosecco and popsicles are items you can buy at the beginning of summer and keep in the freezer and refrigerator until you need them—no rotting, spoiling, or going bad.

The point is to keep it laid back for this impromptu gathering—no wine-glass fountain pyramids or bartenders in vests, m'kay?

For your one food, go for something that's fine served at room temperature, such as watermelon, chips, popcorn, Little Debbies, cherries—just something you can dump into a pretty bowl or set on a tray and forget about.

Author Shauna Niequist recently wrote on Instagram that she aspires to "be cheese-board-ready at all times." This is the high-end version of what I subscribe to, which is to always have something edible on hand that's delicious and easy that I'm not embarrassed to serve to my guests.

MEMORABLE DETAILS. If you provide one special thing for your guests to remember, it will take the focus off anything you hope they will forget, such as your overgrown garden, unpulled weeds, or whatever it is you take issue with in your yard. You can accentuate the positive, which will downplay any negatives simply by providing one thing that grabs the attention of your guests.

The attention-grabbing detail could double as an activity, such as sparklers, light sticks, leftover fireworks, a baby pool or a teepee for the kids. Maybe you set up a cornhole game, croquet, or a telescope for a starry night.

The last-minute, outdoor invitation removes almost every excuse we can come up with for not inviting a friend over. Moving the gathering outside puts the focus on nature and the people without our even trying.

Your attention-grabbing detail could also be something that adds ambiance, such as building a bonfire, making s'mores, turning on the twinkle lights, playing background music, or even hanging a bedsheet and watching a projected movie. One unexpected element that surprises and delights will make you feel like a caring host and will make your guests feel cared for.

Your guests won't remember that you have weeds in your yard or that your house needs to be painted. They'll just remember that one special detail.

Y'all, that's it. For your impromptu outdoor invite, you just need to keep these three things in mind:

- Three things for your outdoor space (seating, surface, and comfort)
- Two foods: one drink, one room-temperature food
- One memorable detail

This summer, follow through on your promise to yourself to invite people over. No excuses. No need to wait for some imaginary time when everything in your yard and your house is finished and better. The last-minute, outdoor invitation removes almost every excuse we can come up with for not inviting a friend over. Moving the gathering outside puts the focus on nature and the people without our even trying. It creates an easy, organic, and stress-free atmosphere, and that's the basis of so many summer memories.

THE HOSTING TRINITY FOR SUMMER GATHERINGS

If you are hosting a big Memorial Day barbecue or another large gathering, the usual hosting trinity we've used in every other season also applies to summer. You need to consider the mood, the food, and the people.

Summer Lemonade Bar

Supplies

- Glass decanter to hold the lemonade
- Lemonade (I buy ours from Chick-fil-A, but you are welcome to make homemade lemonade.)
- An abundance of lemon wedges
- Strawberries, blackberries, blueberries (any berry really)
- Crushed ice and an ice bucket
- An abundance of mint leaves for garnish
- Glasses or mason jars to hold lemonade (Sometimes I load the glasses with a sprig of mint and a wedge of lemon ahead of time.)
- Paper straws to make it feel special

Want some extra fanciness? Set out some bottles of sparkling water. I like a ratio of two parts lemonade to one part sparkling water.

Like all of our seasonal drink bars, this is a serve-yourself setup.

The mood is the atmosphere you set at your gathering. If you followed along in the previous chapter, your home is already cool, calm, and collected and features some seasonal supplies, so you are almost there. Now simply focus on three places to add in a little extra. Hosting a baby shower? Maybe hang a clothesline of tiny white onesies on the fireplace mantel and add floral centerpieces on the buffet and the entryway table. The rest of your house already feels inviting and summerized. Having a Fourth of July party? Choose three decorative items to add in, such as red-and-blue streamers, handheld flags stuck in everything from plants to the fruit bowl, and a blue tablecloth.

For the food, no matter what type of gathering you're hosting, by now you know the rule: commit to making only two foods, tops. The rest need to be store bought or others brought. And of course, the one special detail I always like to provide is a lovely drink station. I like to offer one special drink that feels personal and creative, but that doesn't mean I have to slave over it. In the summer, that might be a lemonade bar with cut-up lemons, bowls of berries, mint leaves, and crushed ice (bought from Sonic, because we fancy!).

When we were first married, Chad's aunt Nancy and uncle Mike would host the Fourth of July every year. Uncle Mike would stay up all night and slave over a hot smoker, tending some type of meat with so much care. Do you know what I remember in detail about the Fourth of July? Nancy's lemonade. Sorry, Mike. That lemonade might have been from a mix, I don't know. I didn't care. All I know is that every July Fourth, Nancy set up a table full of thirst-quenching lemonade in a glass decanter with a bowl of cut-up lemons and crushed ice. She made the entire lemonade area a destination, an experience, if you will. I felt like a VIP getting my delicious ice-cold lemonade from this spectacular setup. I'm suddenly so thirsty for it right now, aren't you?

Your guests will remember special details, but they won't remember every detail. Focusing on one well-thought-out drink station points them to what to remember. And they get to enjoy it visually and with their sense of taste.

Finally, consider the people—your guests, yourself, and your own people. I know you've been thinking about your guests already, and by your providing what we've already talked about, they will feel cared for as long as you make sure that you have enough margin left in your day to be present for them when they show up at your house. It's not selfish to consider your state of mind, protecting yourself from too much hustle; it's actually your job so that you can be fully present for your guests. This goes for your own people too: be sure to communicate expectations, time frames, and how happy you are to get to host people, and over time that joy will rub off onto your family.

BEAUTIFULLY IMPERFECT

I've said it before, but it's my job to repeat this so much that you don't forget it. Hosting is never about the host, and hospitality is never about the house. Isn't that a relief?

Hosting and hospitality aren't reserved for people who have immaculate homes, organized lives, and lots of extra time. Hosting is for any of us who choose to prioritize people over things, and relationships over circumstances. You and I are good at that. Now it's time to put it into action. Lucky for us, summer is the best time to ease into opening up and inviting people over, because it's the most casual season with the lowest of expectations.

This summer, open up your home, your yard, and your clean-enough bathroom. Be the friend who goes first and invites people over. You have everything you need because you are an imperfectionist and a Cozy Minimalist. It's time to create beauty, connection, and meaning with more style, less stuff, and more heart, less hustle as you invite people into your lived-in and loved-on home and yard this summer.

HOSTING BASICS

The other day I was at Target and noticed a lovely platter with the word *Grateful* written on it in cursive. I did what I always do when I see something I love—I put it in my cart and then walked around and thought about whether I would really use it.

I ended up deciding against the platter for two reasons. First, even though we should be grateful all year around, it felt very Thanksgivingy and I didn't want to buy a huge platter I would want to use only at Thanksgiving. Second, the words were in the center of the platter, so once food was on it, no one would be able to read it, which kind of defeated the point of that particular platter. I already had plain white platters that would look just like it once covered with food.

No platter for me.

Being purposeful with my serveware has allowed me to create spreads that look pulled together no matter the occasion, even if I'm serving corn dogs and Tater Tots. Because I'm picky about my serveware, my platters, trays, dishes, and stands all make sense together and help my simple food to look elegant and purposeful. And that's the goal—to have serving pieces that work together all year round. That means you don't need seasonally specific stuff. Instead, you want to invest in things you can use at the bridal shower as well as on Thanksgiving and the Fourth of July.

I focus mainly on white and wood pieces and sometimes fill in the gaps with a few things in black, metals, and natural stone. If it doesn't fit into one of those categories, I don't buy it. Trust me, I have bought beautiful pieces that don't fit into that category. (I'm looking at you, Pioneer Woman cake stand in green milk glass.) But they end up feeling like misfits with my existing collection, and I end up not using them.

For color, I rely on the food, fresh flowers, and linens.

When you focus on a few common materials for your serving pieces—no matter what size or shape you need—it will always look cohesive because it's all meant to work together like a little family. This is a very Cozy Minimalist way to stock your cabinet full of things that are guaranteed to work hard for you every day of the year.

I've found that while most of us manage to end up with decorative yard art and door wreaths for every season, we are somehow missing the basics needed for year-round hosting and decorating. I created a list of items that will serve you every day of the year, most in more ways than one.

These are the basics every home should have, like a capsule wardrobe for your home. If you set a few limitations for yourself when it comes to colors and materials, you'll end up with a collection of hosting supplies you can use in any combination for every possible celebration during any season.

You probably already have a lot of this stuff. Just make sure that you can use it all together without it looking like you are serving a luncheon for clowns.

Serviceware

- Assorted platters in various sizes
- Assorted bowls in various sizes
- Eight to twelve place settings of plain dishes (Mine are from Target.)
- Eight to twelve sets of cutlery
- Serving utensils: scoops, ladles, pie server, slotted spoons
- Mugs you aren't embarrassed to use
- Wine glasses
- Regular glasses
- Decanters, pitchers, carafes
- Creamer, sugar bowl, ice bucket
- Bottle opener, corkscrew, wine stopper
- Wooden boards (Not for cutting on but for serving on. You can get one to cut on too if you want.)
- Cake stand with cover
- Tiered stand
- Season neutral tablecloth
- Cloth napkins

- Paper napkins
- Dish towels (that are preserved and pretty to line bread baskets)
- Small bowls
- Bread knife
- Cheese knives
- Beverage tub

Special Pieces That Can Be Mixed with Your Basics
- Vases (narrow mouth and wide mouth, short and tall)
- Planters and baskets
- Candlesticks
- Candles, scented and unscented
- Throws
- Down inserts
- Pillow covers

I hope you enjoy the process of collecting some hosting items that you can use for any occasion. When you create some basic limitations (for me, white, wood, and metal), it makes the hunt fun but also ensures that your serviceware will look like one happy family that's been collected over time. I love scouring antique malls for vintage items, and festivals for handmade lovelies to add to my collection. Over time, as you focus on making sure your home is stocked with the basics, you'll need to add only a few seasonal supplies to create instant atmosphere, and your home will always be minutes away from ready to host.

MY HOUSE THROUGH THE SEASONS

WINTER

SUMMER

ACKNOWLEDGMENTS

Chad, you have never not encouraged me. All my love.

Landis, Cademon, and Gavin, the greatest joy has been watching you grow up. I'm so proud of who you are.

Mom and Dad, I'm so glad you live close enough to pop right over.

Emily and John, Caroline and Greg, John and Marcy, Megan, Karrie, Angela, Mandi, Lisa, Kendra, and the Cigar Club—Tsh, Erin, Sarah, and Sherry—I'm grateful for your friendship and direction in my life.

Sean, Toby, Caleb, Kurt, and Tell, you have helped make our house into a home.

Jenni, Carolyn, Alicia, Robin, Caleb, Brian, Kait, Curt, and Zondervan in general, you are the dreamiest team ever. Truly, I love working with you.

Family in Indiana, Wisconsin, Florida, Texas, South Carolina, and of course, North Carolina, growing up with you defined home and hospitality for me. I have all the best memories.

Wendy, Erin, and Kat, new friends who unknowingly invited us over while I was working on this book, your hospitality was extra special.

Cozy Minimalist Home

More Style, Less Stuff

Myquillyn Smith

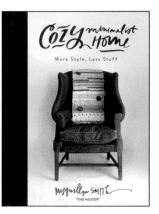

More Style, Less Stuff

Cozy minimalism isn't about going without or achieving a particular new, modern style. Nope. It's simply a mindset that helps you get whatever style YOU LOVE with the fewest possible items.

You want a warm, cozy, inviting home, without using more resources, money, and stuff than needed. Why use more if you don't have to?

In *Cozy Minimalist Home*, accidental stylist and bestselling author Myquillyn Smith guides you step by step on making purposeful design decisions for your home. You'll have the tools to transform your home starting with what you already have, and using just enough of the right furniture and decor to create a home you're proud of in a way that honors your personal priorities, budget, and style. No more fretting when it comes to decorating your house!

In *Cozy Minimalist Home*, Myquillyn Smith helps you

- Realize your role as the curator of your home who makes smart, stylish design choices
- Finally know what to focus on, and what not to worry about when it comes to your home
- Discover the real secret to finding your unique style—it has nothing to do with those style quizzes
- Understand how to find a sofa you won't hate tomorrow
- Deconstruct each room and then recreate it step by step with a failproof process
- Create a pretty home with more style and less stuff, resulting in backward decluttering!
- Finish your home and have it looking the way you've always hoped so you can use it the way you've always dreamed

After reading Myquillyn's first book, *The Nesting Place,* women everywhere were convinced that it doesn't have to be perfect to be beautiful, and they found real contentment in their homes. But how does a content imperfectionist make design decisions?

Cozy Minimalist Home is the answer to that question. Written for the hands-on woman who'd rather move her own furniture than hire a designer, this is the guidance you need to finish every room of your house. With people, priorities, and purpose in mind, anyone can create a beautiful home that transcends the trends.

A pretty home is nice, but a Cozy Minimalist home goes beyond pretty and sets the stage for connection, relationship, and rest.